Blacks in the Humanities, 1750–1984

Recent Titles in
Bibliographies and Indexes in Afro-American and African Studies

Black-Jewish Relations in the United States: A Selected Bibliography
Lenwood G. Davis, compiler

Black Immigration and Ethnicity in the United States:
An Annotated Bibliography
Center for Afroamerican and African Studies, The University of Michigan

Blacks in the American Armed Forces, 1776-1983: A Bibliography
Lenwood G. Davis and George Hill, compilers

Education of the Black Adult in the United States: An Annotated Bibliography
Leo McGee and Harvey G. Neufeldt, compilers

A Guide to the Archives of Hampton Institute
Fritz J. Malval, compiler

A Bibliographical Guide to Black Studies Programs in the United States:
An Annotated Bibliography
Lenwood G. Davis and George Hill, compilers

Wole Soyinka: A Bibliography of Primary and Secondary Sources
James Gibbs, Ketu H. Katrak, and Henry Louis Gates, Jr., compilers

Afro-American Demography and Urban Issues: A Bibliography
R. A. Obudho and Jeannine B. Scott, compilers

Afro-American Reference: An Annotated Bibliography of Selected Resources
Nathaniel Davis, compiler and editor

The Afro-American Short Story: A Comprehensive, Annotated Index with
Selected Commentaries
Preston M. Yancy, compiler

Black Labor in America, 1865-1983: A Selected Annotated Bibliography
Joseph Wilson, compiler and editor

Blacks in the Humanities, 1750-1984

A Selected Annotated Bibliography

Compiled by
Donald Franklin Joyce

Bibliographies and Indexes in Afro-American and African Studies, Number 13

Greenwood Press
New York • Westport, Connecticut • London

Library of Congress Cataloging-in-Publication Data

Joyce, Donald F.
Blacks in the humanities.

(Bibliographies and indexes in Afro-American and African studies, ISSN 0742-6925 ; no. 13)
Includes indexes.
1. Afro-Americans—Bibliography. 2. Humanities—United States—Bibliography. I. Title. II. Series.
Z1361.N39J69 1986 [E185] 016.0013'08996073 86-7600
ISBN 0-313-24643-2 (lib. bdg. : alk. paper)

Library of Congress Catalog Card Number: 86-7600
ISBN: 0-313-24643-2
ISSN: 0742-6925

First published in 1986

Greenwood Press, Inc.
88 Post Road West, Westport, Connecticut 06881

Printed in the United States of America

The paper used in this book complies with the Permanent Paper Standard issued by the National Information Standards Organization (Z39.48-1984).

10 9 8 7 6 5 4 3 2 1

TO

DR. ELIZA ATKINS GLEASON

AND

DR. JOHN HOPE FRANKLIN,

FELLOW FISKITES AND MENTORS
IN A LAND MOST FAIR

Contents

Acknowledgments

This work represents the efforts of many individuals too numerous to cite. However, certain individuals played key roles in assisting me in bringing this project to completion. Dr. Lucius Outlaw, Professor of Philosophy at Haverford College, Dr. Leonard Harris, Professor of Philosophy at Morgan State University, and Dr. Johnny Washington, Professor of Philosophy at the University of Tennessee at Martin, gave valuable advice and direction on Black American contributions in philosophy. Sister Sandra Smithson of Nashville's St. Vincent DePaul Church gave unselfishly of her time and energy in proofreading the entire manuscript for which I will be eternally grateful. University of Illinois Afro-Americana Bibliographer Rosemary Stevenson graciously waded through the many chapters which she received and prepared superb indexes. Wanda Mathews, Reference/Interlibrary Loan Librarian at the Downtown Branch Library of Tennessee State University, should probably have her picture on the cover of this book, having retrieved so many books and photocopies of periodical articles for me to examine in preparing this bibliography. Lillie J. Shelton, Executive Aide in the Office of International Affairs at Tennessee State University, typed and re-typed the manuscript with a smile that was a source of encouragement.

The staff of three libraries were very helpful in their assistance. I am indebted to Ann Allen Shockley, Beth Howse and Dr. Jessie Carney Smith of the Fisk University Library for finding and letting me examine several rare books and journals from the Library's rich Negro collection. The staff of the Jean and Alexander Heard Library of Vanderbilt University assisted me in locating many volumes in their fine collection. And every staff member of the Brown-Daniel Library of Tennessee State University on both campuses cooperated with me in many ways to make this book a reality. Notable among them were Dr. Evelyn P. Fancher, Director; Murle Kenerson, Head of the Reference Department; Fletcher Moon, Reference Librarian; Shirley Caldwell, Head of the Circulation Department; and the entire Circulation Staff.

Acknowledgments

Introduction

Black Americans have made significant contributions to many disciplines in the humanities. Some of these have been documented prominently in several publications, while others have received only passing notice in little-known published and unpublished sources. Blacks in the Humanities, 1750-1984: A Selected Annotated Bibliography relieves students, scholars and researchers of the burden of non-directed searches through the great body of humanistic literature. It is a ready reference guide to major published and unpublished sources in English about the contributions of Black Americans in eleven disciplines of the humanities and a general works category.

Scope and Criteria for Selection

For all humanistic disciplines, sources were selected for inclusion which discuss or document significant contributions by Black Americans to the humanities. The nature of these contributions differ with each discipline. Likewise, the dates of appearance or publication of sources varies, depending on the length of time that Black Americans have been actively making contributions to the various disciplines. Consequently, a criteria has been developed for each discipline and the general works category.

General Works

The general works selected are sources which guide the student or researcher to resources and repositories in Black American cultural and intellectual history that offer the greatest exposure to Black American contributions to the humanities, and document broad achievement by Black Americans in several humanistic disciplines. These sources were published between 1926 and 1984.

Philosophy

Although many Black American intellectual and political leaders have authored works which analyzed the Black experience philosophically, there have been relatively few university-trained Black American philosophers. Prominent among them were Alain L. Locke, William T. Fontaine and Eugene C. Holmes. Most of the literary output of these earlier philosophers was concentrated in periodical literature, although a few authored books. In the 1970s the body of Black American university-trained philosophers began to expand. Like their predecessors, much of the writing of these new Black American philosophers can be found in periodical literature, but an ever-increasing number are writing books. With a few exceptions, the sources cited are by university-trained Black and White American philosophers. They include classic monographs published before 1970 which represent seminal or groundbreaking contributions by Black American philosophers; monographs published since 1970 which are indicative of substantive contributions by contemporary Black American philosophers; selected journal articles by Black American philosophers, which are representative of their myriad interests, and by White American philosophers who address philosophical questions relative to the Black experience; and selected dissertations by Black American philosophers which have been accepted by American universities since 1970 and reflect emerging trends in "doing philosophy" among young Black philosophers.

Religion

The Black American contribution to religion spans almost two decades. The monographic and periodical literature in this discipline is voluminous. There are, however, enduring works which discuss and document major developments and issues in Black American religion as well as the careers of great Black clergy. The works selected are confined to those Black religious institutions which were established by Black Americans within the United States. They include classic monographs published from 1891 through 1960; important treatises published between 1961 and 1984, discussing major contemporary developments in Black religion; periodical articles published after 1979 that discuss major trends in Black religion; and major dissertations accepted by American universities after 1979 which investigate broad topics in Black religion.

Journalism

Published and unpublished sources documenting and discussing Black American activities in newspaper, magazine and radio/television journalism which appeared between 1891 and 1984 are cited. These sources include major bibliographies; indexes to Black newspapers and journals of key historical significance; treatises analyzing and reporting on historical and contemporary developments in Black journalism; biographical works examining the careers and accomplishments of outstanding Black journalists; journal articles, published between 1979 and 1984, which describe contemporary Black involvement in journalism; and unpublished dissertations accepted by American universities from 1980 through 1984 which focus on broadly significant topics involving Black Americans in journalism.

Libraries and Librarianship

Black Americans in libraries and librarianship are represented by forty-one citations. These selected sources are comprised of a directory of Black American librarians and Blacks associated with libraries; major works discussing Black librarianship, library service to Black Americans, and the treatment of materials about Black Americans by librarians; significant studies and commentaries on books, materials and book publishing by and about Blacks; works by Black American librarians on various dimensions of librarianship unrelated to Black Americana; journal articles published between 1936 and 1984 addressing or reporting on key issues, personalities or developments in Black librarianship and Blacks in libraries; and selected dissertations by Black Americans, accepted by American universities between 1980 and 1984, which explore important topics in librarianship and Black American librarianship.

Folklore

A variety of prominent sources exploring several facets of Black American folklore are cited. The works include comprehensive bibliographies listing significant published and unpublished writings on Black American folklore; commentaries and treatises analyzing and discussing specific areas of Black American folklore; studies explicating Black folk medicine, known as Voodoo or Hoodoo; major collections of literature illustrating the Black oral folkloric tradition; current journal articles, published since 1980, which probe and discuss new aspects of Black folklore; and selected dissertations, accepted by American universities in the 1980s, that considernew topics in Black folklore. All of the owrks selected were published or appeared between 1935 and 1984.

Linguistics

Sources selected discussing Black American linguistics appeared from 1928 through 1974. These sources include a comprehensive bibliography; proceedings of major conferences and seminars; dictionaries; treatises and commentaries analyzing specific areas of Black American linguistics; selected journal articles on various subjects in Black American linguistics which were published between 1976 and 1984; and selected dissertations accepted by American universities in the 1980s, representative of new research about Black Americans in this discipline.

Art

Major published and unpublished sources on Afro-American art which appeared from 1916 through 1984 have been selected. They include wide-ranging bibliographies listing a broad array of monographs, exhibit catalogs, dissertations, journal articles and biographical references; indexes to the literature on Black artists and Black art; catalogs of major contemporary exhibitions; treatises discussing and documenting historical and contemporary developments and achievements in Black art; biographical works containing biographies and critiques on the works of Black artists; journal articles, published in the 1980s, which examine particular aspects of contemporary Black art; and dissertations accepted by American universities after 1979 which address original topics in Black art.

Music

The extensive literature on Black music is represented with forty-seven selected sources. They include several exhaustive bibliographies; major discographies on popular, gospel and classical recordings; a yearbook which publishes original research articles in Black music annually, treatises exploring, in-depth, several historical and contemporary developments in Black music; collective biographical works presenting substantive information on a wide variety of Black musicians; journal articles, published between 1980 and 1984, which discuss unique topics in Black music; selected dissertations accepted by American universities since 1979 which are indicative of new genuine contributions to the literature on Black music.

Performing Arts

Citations to fifty-six published and unpublished works in three areas of the performing arts involving Black Americans are included. These areas are drama, film and dance. The types of sources selected were major directories and collective biographies on Black Americans in the performing arts; comprehensive bibliographies and filmographies; the only extant dictionary on the Black theatre in New York City; treatises edamining important aspects of Black drama, Blacks in motion pictures and Black dance; substantive articles in journals discussing Blacks in the performing arts which were published from 1981 through 1984; and dissertations accepted by American universities from 1979 through 1984 which discuss significant aspects of Blacks in the performing arts.

Literary Criticism

The many works on literary criticism of Black literature were examined in an attempt to identify outstanding sources. The works selected, which appeared between 1931 and 1984, are in the following seven categories: major bibliographic reference tools; collective biographical dictionaries that present biographical sketches on major andminor Black writers; special handbooks and indexes providing unique access to specific areas of Black literature; critical literary treatises and commentaries by leading critics of Black literature; substantive critiques on the lives and works of major Black American writers; selected periodical articles, published between 1980 and 1984, which discuss important aspects of Black American literature; and dissertations accepted by American universities which explore groundbreaking topics in Black American literature.

Cultural and Intellectual History

Published and unpublished sources devoted solely to the cultural and intellectual movements among Black Americans have been cited. These works, which dates from 1937 through 1984 include a comprehensive annotated bibliography on the Harlem Renaissance; the first dictionary on terms, personalities, events and works associated with the Harlem Renaissance; published correspondence which discusses intellectual and cultural events in Black America during the twentieth century; an institutional history of the first national Black American scholarly organization in the United States; major treatises discussing Black American cultural and intellectual history; a collective biographical work on Black American historians; selected journal articles, published from 1980 through 1984, on significant subjects in Black American cultural and intellectual history; and a recent dissertation, accepted by an American university, which investigates an important aspect of Black American cultural and intellectual history.

Organization

Blacks in the Humanities, 1750-1984: A Selected Annotated Bibliography is divided into three sections: a selected annotated bibliography, a subject index, and an author-title index.

The selected annotated bibliography is organized into twelve chapters. The first chapter is devoted to general works and the remaining chapters focus on each of the eleven disciplines in the humanities. Each chapter is comprised of sections representing various subjects within the discipline or types of literary formats. For example, in chapter three, "Black Religion: Faith, Hope and Liberation," such sections appear as "Bibliographical Works," "Denominational Histories," "Selected Journal Articles," and "Selected Dissertations."

Each of the twelve chapters is identified consecutively by one of the first twelve letters of the alphabet. For instance, chapter one, "General Works: A Purview," is assigned the letter "A" and chapter three, "Black Religion: Faith, Hope and Liberation," is designated by the letter "C". Within chapters, citations are arranged alphabetically by author or corporate author in each section and are given a numeric/alphabetic code number. The numbers in the code correspond to the citation's numerical position in the chapter and the letter identifies the chapter. Numerical/alphabetic code number (002A) would, therefore, denote the second citation in Chapter A, "General Works: A Purview."

Citations to sources contain the following tiems: author; title; edition, if other than the first edition; place of publication;

publisher; and date. Following the bibliographic entry is a substantiveannotation of the source.

Specific subjects covered in the bibliography are listed alphabetically in the Subject Index. Entries in this index refer to the numbeical/alphabetic code number of the citation. The following is an example:

Specific Subject Entry	Numerical/Alphabetic Code Number
African Methodist Episcopal Church	009C

The reference is to numerical code number (009C) which is the ninth citation in chapter C.

Author and title for sources in the bibliography are arranged alphabetically in the Author-Title Index. Entries in this index refer to the numerical/alphabetic code number of the citation. The following is an example of a citation:

Author-Title Entries	Numerical/Alphabetic Code Number
Blazek, Ron	002A
A Guide to Negro Periodical Literature	006A

In this author entry for "Blazek, Ron," the reference is to numerical/alphabetic code number (002A) which is the second citation in chapter A. For the title entry A Guide to Negro Periodical Literature, the reference is to (006A) which is the sixth citation in chapter A.

Suggestions for Further Research

A review of the published and unpublished literature in the humanities on Arro-Americana reveals a need for additional reference tools and new research studies in many of the humanistic disciplines. A few suggestions follow.

General Works

No new comprehensive annotated bibliographies have appeared on Black Studies since the late 1970s. A comprehensive annotated bibliography on Black Studies citing published and unpublished works which have been completed or appeared since 1980 would greatly facilitate the research of students and scholars in this field.

The extant general encyclopedias in Black Studies are competent reference works for the periods which they cover. Unfortunately, none of these encyclopedias issue annual updates. An encyclopedic yearbook on Black America would fill this vacuum.

Walter Schatz's Directory of Afro-American Resources (031A) is an invaluable reference tool, but it is outdated. Undoubtedly, the collections that the directory covers have added to their holdings since its publication in 1970. A new edition or supplement to the work is needed.

Philosophy

Although fairly recent bibliographies, McClendon (002B) and Harris (003B), have appeared on Blacks in philosophy, a general annotated bio-bibliography in this discipline would greatly encourage new research and give greater visibility to Black American philosophers.

Religion

At present there is no annual published source which contains updated information on the Black church. A yearbook of the Black church would be a welcome addition to the literature on Black religion. Such a reference work might document new developments in the Black church, cite annual statistics, include biographical sketches of the clergy, and list important research articles and books completed on the Black religious institution within the current year.

Journalism

Because more Black Americans are rising to prominence in newspaper, magazine and radio/television journalism, at the regional as well as the national level, there is a need for a dictionary of Blacks in journalism. This work might include biographical sketches of living and deceased Black journalists; statistical information on Black newspaper, magazine and radio/television journalism; directory of Black-owned newspapers, magazine's, and radio/television stations; important dates in Black journalistic history; and synoposes of Black radio/television shows.

Although there are a few dissertations discussing different aspects of the history of Blacks in radio/television journalism, no single source is devoted to a definitive history of this area of Black journalism. A history of Blacks in American radio/television would be a seminal research study in this neglected area of American journalism.

Libraries and Librarianship

Black Americans have been involved in the development of libraries since the late 1820s, when Black literary societies established their own libraries. A history of Blacks in American library development is a neglected subject in American library history which should be documented.

Folklore

A dictionary or encyclopedia of Black American folklore would bean extremely helpful reference tool in this broad ranging discipline. Such a work might include synoposes of major Black folktales, sketches of major folkloric characters, definitions of Black folkloric terms, profiles of folklorists of Black folklore, and commentaries on important works on Black folklore.

Linguistics

A standard resource guide for teachers instructing students who speak Black English should be developed. As reported in the literature on Black English, such a guide for teachers is needed.

Art

The works of Black American artists are housed in many institutions in the United States and abroad. A union catalogue of these works in galleries and other institutions would be a significant addition to Black American art literature.

Music

Black music is a well-documented discipline with several excellent reference tools and treatises. However, one area of Black music history which has been neglected is that of Black-owned opera companies. The literature of Black music history would be greatly enriched by a definitive study of these opera companies.

Performing Arts

An index to Black plays in anthologies, books and other publications is a needed reference tool in Black drama. Such a work would provide greater accessibility to the many plays by Black playwrights.

Black dance is the most under-documented area in the performing arts. A dictionary of Black dance including biographical sketches of Black dancers and teachers, discussions of various types of Black dance, and citations to reviews of Black dance performances would be an important contribution to the literature on Black dance.

Literary Criticism

The literature on Black literary criticism is polific. However, a Black poetry explicator and index to Black short stories are two types of reference works that would aid research efforts in this field.

Cultural and Intellectual History

A reference source which would give greater visibility to Black intellectuals would be a dictionary of Black intellectuals and scholars presenting bio-bibliographic information for those individuals who have made genuine contributions to scholarship. More institutional histories on Black American scholarly societies such as the Association for the Study of Afro-American Life and History should be written. Such organizations are cornerstones of Black American cultural and intellectual history.

Blacks in the Humanities, 1750–1984

A.
General Works: A Purview

GENERAL BIBLIOGRAPHIES, INDEXES AND UNION LISTS

General Bibliographies

(001A) Blacks in America: Bibliographic Essays, by James M. McPherson (and others). Garden City, N. Y.: Doubleday (1973).

This far-ranging work contains critical bibliographical essays by noted historians of the Black experience. The essays cover every phase of Black American history from 1500 to 1970. "Part VIII: Blacks in American Culture, 1900-1970" is devoted to extensive treatment of various aspects of Black American intellectual history. Included in this section are exhaustive bibliographic essays on the following subjects: "The Harlem Renaissance; Exotic Primitivism in the white novel; Fiction of the Renaissance; Jean Toomer and Claude McKay; Black Social Fiction; The 'Protest School'; Black Figures in the Writings of white Southerners: Lillian Smith and William Faulkner; Black Painters and Sculptors; Blacks and the American Theatre; Afro-Americans in Films; South Music: Blues, Jazz and Variations; Blacks in Opera and Symphonic Music; The Black Press Since Booker T. Washington."

(002A) Blazek, Ron and Others. Black Experience: A Bibliography of Bibliographies, 1970-1975. Compiled and edited for the Adult Library Materials Committee, Reference and Adult Services Division, American Library Association. Chicago: American Library Association, 1978.

Several little-known bibliographies and bibliographic essays on a variety of subjects in Black intellectual history are cited in this work. Among some of the subjects treated extensively are: Black english; Black art and artists; historical Black bibliography; Black dance; Black religion; and Black literature.

(003A) Miller, Elizabeth W., Comp. The Negro in America: A Bibliography. Second Edition, Revised and Enlarged. Compiled by Mary L. Fisher. With a New Foreword by Thomas F. Pettigrew. Cambridge, Mass.: Harvard University Press, 1970.

This annotated bibliography of literature about the Black American experience between 1954 and 1969 cites a plethora of selective books and periodical articles relative to Black intellectual history. Such subjects are covered as biography and letters, folklore and literature, theater, dance, and the arts. In a final section entitled "A Guide to Further Research" informative bibliographic essays are included by the compilers to "facilitate more extensive research."

(003.5A) Newman, Richard, comp. Black Access: A Bibliography of Afro-American Bibliographies. Westport, Conn.: Greenwood Press, 1984.

Presenting citations to more than 3,000 bibliographical and discographical works covering many phases of Afro-American culture and history in the United States and Canada, this comprehensive compilation, although the citations are not annotated, is an excellent guide to bibliographies, discographies and related works about Afro-Americans in the humanities and other areas of endeavor. Each bibliography selected was, according to Newman, "included only if it is in some sense 'separately published' that is, it has an independent existence as a book, pamphlet, article, or chapter in a book. The effect has been to exclude all bibliographies that are appendicies to monographs." Citations to bibliographic articles and essays, indexes, book exhibition catalogs, calendars, checklists and guides to manuscripts have, also, been included. To assist the researcher in the study of particular periods in history, this work has a chronological index with entries that indicate inclusive dates that the bibliography described covers. A subject index, composed of key words in each bibliographical, discographical or related work, has been developed to assist the researcher in finding citations on a particular subject.

(004A) Peavy, Charles D. Afro-American Literature and Culture Since World War II: A Guide to Information Sources. (American Studies Information Guide Series, Vol. 6). Detroit: Gale, 1979.

Part I of this annotated bibliography covers twenty-eight areas of the Black experience including twelve specialized subjects in Black intellectual history. Part II, devoted to Black writers, contains bibliographies of the works and criticism of each author.

(005A) Work, Monroe. A Bibliography of the Negro in Africa and America. New York: H. W. Wilson, 1928.

This pioneering bibliography was the most comprehensive work of its kind to appear in the first fifty years of the twentieth century. Containing over 17,000 entries for monographs, periodicals and pamphlets in English and several foreign languages, it is an indispensable index to much of the early literature in Black intellectual history.

General Indexes

(006A) A Guide to Negro Periodical Literature. Vols. 1-4, no. 3. Compiled by A. P. Marshall. Winston-Salem, N. C.: A. P. Marshall, 1941-1946. Quarterly.

This is the only work indexing Black journals and periodicals during the period covered. For articles in Black periodicals and journals on every area of Black intellectual history during this period it is an essential source.

(007A) Index to Periodical Articles By and About Negroes. Boston: G. K. Hall, 1950-

Formerly entitled Index to Selected Periodicals on the Negro, this source indexes more Black periodicals and journals than any other index. Included in its subject arrangements are all areas of Black cultural and intellectual history.

(008A) Spradling, Mary Mace, ed. In Black and White: A Guide to Magazine Articles, Newspaper Articles and Books Concerning More than 15,000 Black Individuals and Groups. Third edition. Detroit: Gale, 1980. 2 vols.

A valuable resource for information on the achievements by Blacks from the late 18th century to 1979, this index is arranged into three sections. Section I lists individuals and organizations with references to items about them in books, periodicals, and newspapers. Section II is an index to individuals arranged by occupations. Section III lists books, magazines and newspapers which included information on prominent Blacks.

Union Lists

(009A) The Chicago Afro-American Union Analytic Catalog: An Index to Materials on the Afro-American in the Principal Libraries of Chicago. Boston: G. K. Hall, 1972. 5 v.

This annotated catalog, compiled by the Works Progress Administration, contains over 75,000 analytical entries to books, periodicals, pamphlets, and other materials, excluding newspapers, on every aspect of the Black experience from the late 18th century to 1940 in the principla libraries of Chicago. Arranged by author, title and subject, every aspect of Afro-American life and history is covered. Over 1,000 foreign and domestic journals and periodicals are indexed and analyzed.

(010A) Matthews, Geraldine O. Black American Writers, 1773-1949: A Bibliography and Union List. Compiled by Geraldine O. Matthews and the Staff of the African-American Materials Project. Boston: G. K. Hall, 1975.

Cataloging the monographs of more than 1600 Black authors held in the libraries of six southeastern states, this unique work focuses on pre-1950 imprints. Each citation is annotated. Arranged by broad subject, the following aspects of Black intellectual history are included: philosophy; language; fine arts; literature and history. For the majority of citations, library location symbols are given.

ENCYCLOPEDIAS

(011A) The Black American Reference Book. Edited by Mabel M. Smythe. Sponsored by the Phelps-Stokes Fund. Englewood Cliffs, N. J.: Prentice-Hall, 1976.

This one volume work contains authoritative articles on many aspects of Black American life by noted scholars and specialists. Ten chapters are devoted to subjects relative to Black intellectual history. Among some of them are: "Afro-American Religion," by Henry V. Richardson and Nathan Wright, Jr.; "Afro-American Music," by Wendell Whalum, David Baker, and Richard Long; and "Afro-American Art," by Edmund B. Gaither.

(012A) International Library of Afro-American Life and History. Cornwells Heights, Pa.: The Publishers Agency, Inc. under the auspices of the Association for the Study of Afro-American Life and History, 1978. 10 vols.

This ten-volume encyclopedia contains articles, excerpts for original works, and critical commentaries on many facets of Afro-American life and history. The following three volumes focus on major aspects of Black intellectual history: The Negro in Music and Art; comp. by Lindsay Patterson (1978); Anthology of the Afro-American in the Theatre: A Critical Approach, comp. by Lindsay Patterson (1978); An Introduction to Black Literature in America from 1746 to the Present, comp. by Lindsay Patterson (1978).

BIOGRAPHICAL DICTIONARIES

(013A) Dictionary of American Negro Biography. Edited by Rayford W. Logan and Michael R. Winston. New York: Norton, 1982.

Similar in format to the Dictionary of American Biography, this biographical dictionary contains substantive biographies on prominent Black Americans who were deceased before January 1, 1970. Written by noted scholars and specialists, each biography includes a bio-bibliography on the biographee.

(014A) Who's Who Among Black Americans. Edited by William C. Matney. Third edition, 1980-81. Northbrook, Ill.: Who's Who Among Black Americans, Inc. Publishing Co., 1981.

Including biographical entries on living Black Americans who have made significant achievements in American life, this biographical dictionary is the major source of reference for living prominent Black Americans.

(015A) Robinson, Wilhelmena S. Historical Afro-American Biographies, 1979 ed. Cornwells Heights, Pa.: Publishers Agency, 1978. (International Library of Afro-American Life and History.)

This useful reference source contains substantial biographical sketches on Blacks from the fourteenth century through the twentieth century. Its extensive bibliography includes citations in maps and journals on all biographies.

LIBRARY CATALOGS

(016A) Bell and Howell. Atlanta University. Black Culture Collection of Atlanta University. Cleveland: Bell and Howell, 1971. 4 v.

This catalog, which accesses the Atlanta University Black Collection that is available on microfilm, is an index to one of the major collections on Black history in the United States. Including over 6,000 titles, this Collection is very strong in primary and secondary sources in Black intellectual history from 1930 to the present.

(017A) Chicago Public Library. Dictionary Catalog of the Vivian G. Harsh Collection of Afro-American History and Literature. Boston: G. K. Hall, 1978. 4 v.

Containing over 28,000 titles covering every phase of Afro-Americana, this collection is very strong in Afro-American intellectual history in the following areas: history, art, philosophy and literature. Included in its manuscripts unit are works by Richard Wright, Langston Hughes and thirty-five other Black writers.

(018A) Detroit Public Library. Catalog of the E. Azalia Hackley Memorial Collection of Negro Music, Dance and Drama. Boston: G. K. Hall, 1979.

The core of this collection is the personal library of E. Azalia Hackley, a noted Black musician and music teacher. The collection documents the achievements of Blacks in music, dance, theatre, motion pictures and broadcasting. It includes musical scores, books, broadsides, posters, photographs, phonograph records and clippings.

(019A) Fisk University Library. Dictionary Catalog of the Negro Collection of the Fisk University Library. Boston: G. K. Hall, 1974. 6 v.

One of the most extensive collections of materials on Black history, this collection is particularly strong in primary sources in Black intellectual history. Among some of its rich manuscript collections on the subject are: The Charles Wadell Chestnutt Papers; The Countee Cullen Papers; The Pauline Hopkins Papers; The Langston Hughes Papers; The Charles Spurgeon Johnson Papers; The Scott Joplin Papers; and The Jean Toomer Papers.

(020A) Hampton Institute. Collis P. Huntington Library. Dictionary Catalog of the George Peabody Collection of Negro History and Literature. Westport, Conn.: Greenwood Press, 1972. 2 v.

This sizeable collection, 11,000 volumes, covers many phases of the Black experience in America. Notable among its manuscript collections relative to Black intellectual history are The Papers of R. Nathaniel Dett, composer-arranger.

(021A) Howard University Library. The Dictionary Catalog of the Jessie E. Moorland Collection of Negro Life and History. Boston: G. K. Hall, 1970. 6 v.

Suppl. Boston: G. K. Hall, 1976. 3 v.

One of the richest repositories on Black history in the United States, this Collection has the personal papers of many of the figures in Black intellectual history. Among some of them are: The Papers of E. Franklin Frazier, sociologist; The Papers of Alain Locke, philosopher; and The Papers of James Porter, art historian.

(022A) Howard University Library. The Dictionary Catalog of the Arthur B. Spingarn Collection of Negro Authors. Boston: G. K. Hall, 1970. 2 v.

Housed in the Howard University Library, this Collection reflects the collecting efforts of Arthur B. Spingarn, one of the noted collectors of literature by Black authors in the world. Including only Black authors, this collection is extremely rich in many of the works of Black scholars and writers prominent in Black intellectual history.

(023A) New York Public Library. Schomburg Collection of Negro Literature and History. Dictionary Catalog of the Schomburg Collection of Negro Literature and History. Boston: G. K. Hall, 1962. 9 vols.

Suppl. I. Boston: G. K. Hall, 1967. 2 vols.

Suppl. II. Boston: G. K. Hall, 1974. 4 vols.

One of the largest centers in the world for the study of Black history, this collection includes works in many formats relative to Black intellectual history such as books, manuscripts, periodicals, newspapers, microforms, oral history tapes, sheet music, and institutional archives. Notable among papers and manuscripts of prominent Black American intellectuals housed in the collection are: the John Edward Bruce Papers; the Alexander Crummell Papers; the Oakley C. Johnson Papers; the Rose McClendon Papers and the William Pickens Papers.

(024A) Bibliographic Guide to Black Studies. Boston: G. K. Hall, 1975-

Published annually, this catalog lists new book acquisitions in the Schomburg Collection.

HISTORICALLY SIGNIFICANT AND RELEVANT COMPILATIONS AND COLLECTIONS

(025A) Cunard, Nancy, comp. Negro: An Anthology. Edited and abridged, with an introduction by Hugh Ford. New York: F. Ungar Pub. Co., 1970.

Originally published in 1934 at her own expense by Nancy Cunard, the wealthy heiress of the British-based Cunard Steamship Lines, to prove that there was no superior race, this work is the most comprehensive collective expression of Black intellectual inquiry to appear in the first fifty years of the twentieth century. Contemporary leading Black intellectuals from practically every area of humanities are represented in essays, poems, commentaries and other literary genre.

(026A) Porter, Dorothy Barnett, comp. Early Negro Writing, 1760-1837. Selected and introduced by Dorothy Barnett Porter. Boston: Beacon Press, 1971.

A far-ranging and important compilation of many of the most significant writings and documents emanating from Black Americans during the period covered, this work is an invaluable index to early Black American intellectual thought. It is divided into the following sections: "Part I: Mutual Aid and Fraternal Organizations, 1792-1833;" "Part II: Societies for Educational Improvement, 1808-1836;" "Part III: Significant Annual Conferences, 1831-1837;" "Part IV: To Emigrate or Remain at Home? 1773-1833;" "Part V: Spokesmen in Behalf of Their Colored Fellow Citizens;" "Part VI: Saints and Sinners, 1786-1836;" "Part VII: Narratives, Poems and Essays, 1760-1835."

(027A) Woodson, Carter G., ed. The Mind of the Negro As Reflected in Letters Written During the Crisis, 1800-1860. Washington, D. C.: Association for the Study of Negro Life and History, 1926.

This work is one of the broadest barometers of the intellectual life of Black Americans in antebellum America. Written by free Blacks, these letters document the intellectual responses of literate individuals on a variety of topical subjects.

(028A) Woodson, Carter G. ed. Negro Orators and Their Orations. Washington, D.C.: Associated Publishers, 1925.

Containing many of the important speeches by Black Americans which had appeared in print from the early 1800s through 1922, this collection provides insight into the minds of leading Black Americans for the period covered.

CLASSIC ORGANIZATIONAL AND INSTITUTIONAL PUBLICATIONS

(029A) American Negro Academy. Occasional Papers, Nos. 1-22. Washington, D. C.: The Academy, 1897-1914. (Reprint, New York: Arno Press and the New York Times, 1969).

Founded in 1897 by Alexander Crummell, the prolific nineteenth century clergyman and intellectual, the American Negro Academy, whose membership included the leading Black American intellectuals and writers of the day, published annually between 1897 and 1922 substantive papers authored by its members. Among some of the publications were: The Negro and his Citizenship, by Rev. F. J. Frimke; The Status of the Negro from 1800 to 1870, by L. M. Henshaw; and American Negro Bibliography of the Past, by J. W. Chestnutt.

(030A) Atlanta University. Atlanta University Publications, Nos. 1-20. Atlanta: Atlanta University Press, 1896-1916. (Reprint, New York: Arno Press and the New York Times, 1970).

A landmark endeavor in the intellectual history of the Black America, the Atlanta University Publications, regarded by many scholars as the earliest researches in urban sociology conducted in the South, were the results of annual conferences held at Atlanta University from 1896 to 1918. Between 1897 and 1910, these studies were directed by W. E. B. DuBois. They include such studies as: No. 1 - Mortality Among Negroes in the Cities (1896); No. 2 - Social and Physical Conditions of Negroes in Cities (1897); and No. 3 - Some Efforts of American Negroes for Their Own Social Betterment (1898).

DIRECTORIES

(031A) Schatz, Walter, ed. Directory of Afro-American Resources. Race Relations Information Center. New York: R. R. Bowker, 1970.

Citing the holdings of Afro-Americana in 5,365 collections in the United States, this source provides comprehensive descriptions of Afro-Americana in public, private, college and university libraries. Entries for each repository focus on the book, manuscript and non-book holdings. Excellent subject and name indexes are extremely helpful to researchers in Black intellectual history.

B.
Homage to Alain Locke: Blacks in Philosophy

DIRECTORIES

(001B) Outlaw, Lucius T., Comp. International Directory of Philosophers of African Descent. Haverford, PA: Department of Philosophy, Haverford College, 1983. (Studies in Africana Philosophy).

Philosophers of African descent, living in nineteen countries, who have formal training in philosophy are included in this pioneering directory. Arranged alphabetically by country and sub-arranged alphabetically by philosophers residing within the country, each entry includes the name, address and, in many entries, the educational attainment of the philosopher.

BIBLIOGRAPHICAL WORKS

(002B) McClendon, John H., Comp. Afro-American Philosophers and Philosophy: A Selected Bibliography. Urbana, IL: University of Illinois, Afro-American Studies and Research Program, 1981. (Afro Scholar Working Papers, No. 7).

Covering Afro-American involvement in philosophy from the late 19th century through 1980, this wide-ranging bio-bibliography, including living and deceased Afro-Americans who engaged in doing philosophy, is divided into five sections. They are: (A) Major Black Philosophers; (B) Practicing Black Philosophers; (C) Professionally Trained-Black Philosophers; (D) Contemporary Black Philosophers: Directory and Selected Bibliography; and (E) Philosophical Analysis of the Black Experience. Sections A, B, and C contain biographical sketches of Black philosophers with bibliographies of their published and unpublished works. Section D lists contemporary Black philosophers, their addresses, educational training and, in many instances, published and unpublished works. Section D is a selected bibliography of works which analyze the Black experience philosophically.

(003B) "Select Bibliography of Afro-American Works in Philosophy," by Leonard Harris. (In Harris, Leonard. Philosophy Born of

Struggle: Anthology of Afro-American Philosophy from 1917. Dubuque, Iowa: Kendall/Hunt, 1983, pp. 289-315).

Although unannotated and excluding the works of Frederick Douglass, Alexander Crummell, Marcus Garvey, W. E. B. DuBois, C. L. R. James and Dr. Martin L. King, this is one of the most extensive bibliographies to appear on Afro-American scholars in the humanities, the majority of whom are professionally-trained philosophers, The works, which ranged in publication dates from 1892 through 1982, include monographs, journal articles, book reviews and unpublished dissertations.

GENERAL WORKS

(004B) Harris, Leonard, ed. Philosophy Born of Struggle: Anthology of Afro-American Philosophy from 1917. Dubuque, IA: Kendall/Hunt, 1983.

Professor Harris has collected in this anthology twenty-one major articles and essays on Black philosophy by Black scholars and philosophers which were published since 1917, the year Dr. Alain Locke became the chairperson of the Department of Philosophy at Howard University and developed it into the springboard for many Black philosophers. The knowledgeable introduction by Harris describes the historical development of professional philosophy among Black Americans from the late nineteenth century to 1981. One of the excellent features of the work is the comprehensive bibliography, citation (003B). Among the classic works included are: "Social Determinism in the writings of Negro Scholars," by William T. Fontaine; Frederick Douglass: The Black Philosopher in the United States: A Commentary," by Broadus N. Butler; "Values and Imperatives," by Alain L. Locke; and "Ethics and Moral Activism," by Cornelius L. Golightly.

(005B) James, George G. M. Stolen Lagacy. Introduction by Asa G. Hilliard. New York: Philosophical Library, 1954. (Reprint: San Francisco: Julian Richardson Associates, 1976).

Most scholars believe that Western philosophy originated in Greece. In this heavily documented work, James attempts to show that the Greeks borrowed many of their philosophical concepts from the Africans, namely the Egyptians. The Memphite theology, James asserts, is the basis of Greek philosophy.

(006B) National Council for Black Studies. Sixth Annual Conference, Chicago, 1982. Proceedings No. 3: Philosophical Perspectives in Black Studies. Edited by Gerald A. McWhorter. Urbana: University of Illinois, Afro-American Studies and Research Program, 1982.

Papers presented by seven outstanding Black philosophers and scholars on different aspects of Black philosophy are included in this set of the Proceedings of the Sixth Annual Conference of the National Council for Black Studies. The papers are: "Philosophy in Africa and The African Diaspora: Contemporary African Philosophy," by Lucius T. Outlaw; "Haitian Intellectual Currents: The Struggle for Identity," by Patrick Bellegarde-Smith; "Social Class in Drake and Cayton's Black Metropolis: Reflections on a Text in the Classical Tradition of Afro-American Scholarship," by Glenn H. Jordan; "Philosophy Born of Struggle: Afro-American Philosophy from 1918," by Leonard Harris; "Afro-centricity -- Does It Lead to Black Liberation," by Deborah Atwater-Hunter; "Black Religion: Its Significance for Black Studies," by John L. Jackson; "Eugene Clay Holmes: A Commentary on a Black Marxist Philosopher," by John H. McClendon.

TEXTBOOKS AND TEACHING AIDS IN PHILOSOPHY

(007B) Banner, William A. Ethics: An Introduction to Moral Philosophy. New York: Scribner's, 1968.

Using the historical-topical approach, this useful textbook provides a sound introduction to moral philosophy. Banner discusses representative moral philosophies such as Greek Ethics, Christian Ethics, Utilitarianism and Existentialism. In the concluding chapter, the concepts of freedom and responsibility are analyzed.

(008B) Frye, Charles A., ed. Level Three: A Black Philosophy Reader. Lanham, MD: University Press of America, 1980.

Designed for undergraduate students, this collection of writings in philosophy by Black and white philosophers and scholars explores the concept of "A Worldview of Blackness" on three structured levels. Level One examines the economic, political and social history of Black people. Level Two explores the arts, literature, sociology and linguistics of the Black experience, and Level Three, focusing on religion and philosophy, discusses the meaning of the Black experience.

(009B) Hickey, Dennis, ed. Black Contemporary Philosophy. Pasadena, CA: Williams and Williams, 1971.

This volume, conceived as a teaching aid for undergraduate students in philosophy, presents the philosophical views of sixteen successful professional Blacks residing in Southern California. These views were obtained through structured interviews conducted by a philosophy professor. Among some of the questions asked in the interview were: "What is the ultimate goal of human existence?; What is the basis of motality?; Is man fundamentally free?"

(010B) Hill, Charles Leander. A Short History of Modern Philosophy from Renaissance to Hegel. Boston: Meador Publishing Co., 1951.

Written by philosopher Charles Leander Hill when he was President of historically-Black Wilberforce University, this work is one of the earliest textbooks on classical philosophy authored by a Black American. Aimed at undergraduate students in the history of philosophy, it is an exposition of the philosophical systems of major Western philosophers from Bacon to Hegel.

(011B) Johnston, Percy E. Afro-American Philosophers: Selected Readings from Jupiter Hammon to Eugene C. Holmes. Upper Montclair, NJ: Montclair State College Press, 1970.

The philosophical thoughts of twenty Black American philosophers, writers and scholars from the late eighteenth century through the 1960s are presented in excerpts from their writings and speeches in this anthology. Intended for undergraduate students in philosophy, the selections are aimed at introducing the reader to the historical development of Black American philosophy. Some of the excerpts from works included are: "A General Theory of the Freedom Cause of the Negro People," by Eugene C. Holmes; and "The Negro as an Industrial Makeshift," by Marcus Garvey. An excellent selected annotated bibliography on Black American thought and philosophy is included.

(012B) Okadigbo, Chuba; Baltazar, Eulalio. Logic for Black Undergraduates. Dubuque, IA: Kendall/Hunt, 1974.

The basic principles of logic, illustrated with examples drawn from the Black experience, are presented in this unique textbook designed for Black as well as white undergraduate students in philosophy. Each of the twelve chapters in the textbook are devoted to such specific topics as: "Deductive Reasoning; The Categorical Syllogism; and Obversion and Conversion." Within each chapter there are exercises, utilizing a variety of experiences from Black life, constructed to test the student's understanding of principles presented in the chapter.

SELECTED PHILOSOPHICAL TREATISES ON RACE AND RACE RELATIONS

(013B) Boxhill, Bernard R. Blacks and Social Justice. Totowa, NJ: Bowman & Allanheld, 1984.

Race relations policies in the United States have grown less liberal in the 1980s than they had been in the 1970s. The Reagan Administration has adopted highly conservative positions on busing, affirmative action and housing discrimination. Professor Boxhill analyzes and discusses from a philosophical perspective such "color conscious" governmental policies as preferential policies, affirmative action and busing in an attempt to rebut the logic and philosophical assumptions of the critics of these policies. He effectively challenges such critics as Thomas Sowell and Ronald Dworkins.

(014B) Davis, Angela. Women, Race and Class. New York: Random House, 1981.

Angela Davis, in this work, indicts "Monopoly Capitalism" for the exploitation of Black women. Attempting to advance the cause of socialism, Davis analyzes the history of the Women's

Movement. She exposes the racist shortcomings of its leaders towards Black Americans and concludes that, because the Women's Movement has been confined to the white middle class, it lacks potential for effecting any real revolutionary change.

(015B) *Fontaine, William T. Reflections on Segregation, Desegregation, Power and Morals. Springfield, IL: Charles C. Thomas, 1967.

After analyzing the state of race relations in the United States in the mid-1960s, this Black philosopher attempts to clarify the major issues involved and points the way to a new program of action. He achieves this two-fold objective by: (1) citing the changing aspirations of Black Americans since Reconstruction; (2) elucidating the many problems related to segregation and desegregation; (3) analyzing reasons why many white Americans want desegregation; (4) assessing housing as the most crucial problem in establishing de facto segregation and suggesting ways in which philanthrophy can assist in overcoming it; and (5) critiquing the Black Power concept.

(016B) Frye, Charles A., ed. Values in Conflict: Blacks and the American Ambivalence Toward Violence. Washington, D. C.: University of America, 1980.

Violence in American life, focusing on Black Americans, is the theme of these essays by philosophers, theologians and educators which were originally presented as papers at a symposium at Fayetteville State University in 1978. The following aspects of violence are discussed: "The American Ambivalance Towards Violence; The Image of the Bad Man in America; The Roots of Violence; and Controlled Violence."

(017B) Hodge, John L.: Struckmann, Donald K.; Trost, Lynn Dorland. Cultural Basis of Racism and Group Oppression. Berkeley, CA: Two Riders Press, 1975.

In this philosophical examination of traditional "Western" concepts, values, and institutional structures which support racism, sexism and elitism, the authors identify and discuss the intellectual assumptions in Western thought and culture which have initiated and continue to perpetuate these forms of oppression. This oppression is both external, Westerners dominating Non-Westerners, and internal, Westerners dominating Westerners as evidence by sexism and economic domination. By examining these basic causes of oppression, the authors hope that they have begun part of the process of creating alternative ways of life which can benefit all of the world's people.

SELECTED TREATISES ON MORAL, POLITICAL AND HISTORICAL PHILOSOPHY

(018B) Banner, William A. Moral Norms and Moral Order: The Philosophy of Human Affairs. Gainesville, FL: University of Florida Presses, 1981.

Aristotle thought that discourses into ethics and politics had the same duty: to explain moral nobility and justice. In this broad and esoteric treatise, Howard University Philosopher, William A. Banner, is in agreement with Aristotle. He systematically explores the issues related to morality and its regulation, focusing on the rights and duties of the individual in an organized society.

(019B) Eddins, Berkley B. Appraising Theories of History. Cincinnatti: Ehling, 1980.

After presenting a general discussion of the philosophy of history, Eddins critically assesses the grand philosophies of history advanced by Arnold Toynbee and Oswald Spengler. He concludes by formulating a criteria for evaluating a philosophy of history.

(020B) James, C. L. R. Notes on Dialectics: Hegel and Marxism. Detroit: Facing Reality Publications, 1971.

Regarded as James' most definitive philosophical work, Notes on Dialectics is an analysis of his intellectual response to Hegel and Marx. It is in this treatise that James discusses his anti-Leninist views.

(021B) Locke, Alain L. "Values and Imperatives." (In Kallen, Horace M. and Hook, Sidney, eds. American Philosophy Today and Tomorrow. New York: Furman, 1935), pp. 313-333.

Locke begins this classic essay, which was published in 1935, by criticizing American philosophers for neglecting to consider in-depth value analysis. He observes:

> "Though they have at times discussed the problems of value, they have usually avoided their normative aspects..."

Arguing from the premise that man does not live in a valueless world, Locke carefully discusses his value theory stressing the need for absolutes and imperatives.

AESTHETICS

(022B) Locke, Alain L., ed. New Negro: An Interpretation. New York: A. C. Boni, 1925.

This collection of essays, fiction, poetry and art work by the leading figures in the Harlem Renaissance, celebrating artistically and intellectually many facets of Afro-American life, is a watershed in Afro-American cultural and intellectual history. Philosopher Alain Locke, intellectual father of the cultural aspects of the Harlem Renaissance, in his introductory essay based on his concept of cultural pluralism, brilliantly interprets the Renaissance as the flowering of Afro-American culture.

AUTOBIOGRAPHICAL WORKS

(023B) Davis, Angela. Angela Davis: An Autobiography. New York: Random House, 1974.

Philosopher Angela Davis, in this autobiography, offers rare insight into the growth and development of a young Black philosopher in America in the 1950s and 1960s. She recounts her childhood in Alabama, family life, education and political life. Her years under the guidance of Herbert Marcuse show his influence on her subsequent development as a philosopher and political theorist.

(024B) Washington, Johnny. Alain Locke and Philosophy: A Quest for Cultural Pluralism. Westport, CT: Greenwood Press, 1985.

The first Afro-American Rhodes Scholar and a Harvard-trained doctorate in philosophy, Alain Locke became the leading Afro-American philosopher in the first half of the twentieth century. Locke's concepts of cultural pluralism and value relativism are the focus of this premier intellectual biography of the celebrated Black philosopher. Washington discusses and analyzes in detail Locke's writings and activities as cultural interpreter of the Black experience as well as a Black educator.

SIGNIFICANT JOURNAL ARTICLES

(025B) Axelsen, Diana. "With All Deliberate Delay: On Justifying Preferential Policies in Education and Employment." Philosophical Forum 9 (Winter-Spring, 1977-78); 264-288.

The implementation of affirmative action programs and preferential policies has, in many quarters, polarized racial and sexist attitudes in the United States today. Dr. Axelsen in this essay discusses some of the philosophical values relative to preferential policies, cites criticisms voiced against them, and presents arguments which support them. She concludes by pointing out that a possible justification for these policies can be based on the rights of individuals and groups for past as well as present injustices.

(026B) Boxhill, Bernard R. "How Justice Pays." Philosophy and Public Affairs. 9 (Summer 1980):359-71.

Boxhill argues in this essay that the case for the doctrine that justice is profitable and injustice unprofitable is self-defeating. He concludes that the doctrine is a dangerous falsehood.

(027B) Cook, Joyce M. "The Nature and Nurture of Intelligence. The Philosophical Forum 9 (Winter-Spring, 1977-78).

The IQ controversy, focusing on racial differences continues to spark interchange among intellectuals from many disciplines. Philosopher Joyce Cook, after discussing several questions on the interpretation of raw data by psychologists, analyzes the alledged influence of racism on the IQ controversy.

(028B) Davis, Angela."Rape Racism and the Capitalist Setting." Black Scholar 12 (November/December 1981):2-15.

Angela Davis discusses the pervasiveness of rape as a violent crime in capitalist countries, especially the United States. Focusing on the role of racism in rape cases, Davis notes that most rape laws are designed to protect upper class white men and to convict Black men who, between 1963 and 1967, comprised 405 out of 455 men executed for rape.

(029B) Golightly, Cornelius L. "A Philosopher's View of Values and Ethics." Personnel and Guidance Journal 50(December 1971):289-294.

Aimed at professional counselors, this essay discusses, from a philosopher's point of view, the theoretical framework in which counselors may make rational decisions about values in their counseling practice. The author concludes that: "values arise out of our beliefs and desires."

(030B) Hill, Eric. "Hume and the Delightful Tragedy Problem." Philosophy. 57(July 1982):319-26.

In his essay "of Tragedy," David Hume discusses the ironic pleasure spectators experience while watching a well-written tragedy. Eric Hill attempts in this article to analyze Hume's discussion of tragedy in an effort to determine whether Hume's perception of tragedy is adequate.

(031B) Holmes, Eugene C. "The Main Philosophical Considerations of Space and Time." American Journal of Physics 18(December 1950):560-570.

In this landmark essay, Holmes examines the philosophical formulations related to space and time in the work of several philosophers from the Ionians to the neo-Kantians. Among some of the philosophers discussed are Galileo, Gassendi, Descartes, Kant, Schlick, and Carnap.

(032B) Jones, William R. "The Legitimacy and Necessity of Black Philosophy: Some Preliminary Considerations." Philosophical Forum 9(Winter-Spring 1977-8):149-160.

Many critics question the legitimacy of Black philosophy. In this essay, Jones refutes four of the most common criticisms launched against the legitimacy of Black philosophy. They are: (1) philosophy is universal and, therefore, has no color; subsequently, it is inappropriate to attach qualifiers to it such as Black, red or feminist because they denature it; (2) ethnic philosophies are self-refuting; (3) advocates of Black philosophy confuse ontological and sociological categories; and (4) there is no foundation for Black philosophy as there is for Jewish philosophy and

Black theology.

(033B) Kelly, Derek A. "Philosophy of R. Buckminister Fuller." International Philosophical Quarterly. 22(December 1982): 295-414.

R. Buckminister Fuller has been called a genius. He has distinguished himself as a novelist, scientist, engineer, architect, poet and philosopher. Although he disagrees with many of Fuller's philosophical ideas, Kelly presents in this essay a systematic interpretation of Fuller's philosophical views.

(034B) McClendon, John H. "The Afro-American Philosopher and the Philosophy of the Black Experience: A Bibliographical Essay on a Neglected Topic in Both Philosophy and Black Studies." Sage Race Relations Abstracts 7(November 1982): 1-52.

In this comprehensive bibliographical essay McClendon discusses works by Afro-American philosophers and the philosophical works on the Black experience by Afro-American intellectuals, writers and specialists from other disciplines. The following five areas are examined: (1) philosophical reference materials; (2) philosophies on the Black experience; (3) axiology; (4) philosophy of history; and (5) philosophy of science.

(035B) McClendon, John H. "Dr. Holmes, the Philosopher Rebel." Freedomways 22(Spring 1982):44-51.

Eugene C. Holmes, although relatively unknown, was one of the major Black American Philosophers during the first six decades of the twentieth century. McClendon discusses Holmes' contribution to Black intellectual history and shows that, philosophically, Holmes was a dialectical materialist.

(036B) McDage, Jesse N. "Toward An Antology of Negritude." Philosophical Forum 9(Winter-Spring 1977-78):161-167.

Philosophically, is there such a reality as the Black perspective? Professor McDade responds to this question by: (1) briefly discussing the development of Negritude; (2) evaluating critically Sartre's assessment of Negritude; (3) discussing five ontological assumptions; and (4) analyzing passages from Kant's Critique of Pure Reason in a rather successful effort to lay groundwork for an ontology of Negritude.

(037B) McGary, Howard, Jr. "Justice and Reparations." Philosophical Forum 9(Winter-Spring, 1977-78):250-263.

When James Foreman raised the issue of Black reparations during services at New York City's Riverside Church in 1969, he demanded that Black Americans receive 50 million dollars in reparations for unjust treatment that their ancestors had suffered in America. In this essay Professor McGary examines the philosophical justification for reparations as a concept of social justice. He alludes to John Locke and other social contract theorists in support of his argument.

(038B) Murundi, John. "Toward an Understanding of African Art." Diogenes 119(Fall 1982):114-31.

An invitation to an understanding of African Art is a process, Murundi states, which involves the whole being of man. Murundi describes and analyzes the process in this essay.

(039B) Popkini, Richard H. "Hume's Racism." Philosophical Forum 9(Winter-Spring 1977-78):211-226.

Although David Hume was a critic of superstition and prejudice, he was a racist. In several of his discussions on race, he attempted to justify the superiority of whites and the inferiority of Blacks. This essay discusses Hume's theorizing on race.

(040B) Simpson, Lorenzo C. "A Critical Note Concerning Marcuse's Theory of Science." Philosophy of the Social Sciences]3(1983):451-63.

Philosopher Herbert Marcuse has advanced the proposition that modern science is inherently technological. Simpson challenges Marcuse's proposition on what he believes to be two confusions in Marcuse's thinking.

(041B) Thomas, Laurence. "Ethical Egoism and Psychological Dispositions." American Philosophical Quarterly. 17(January 1980):73-80.

Ethical egotism, as a moral theory, is unacceptable to Lawrence Thomas. In this essay, Thomas explains his position philosophically.

(042B) West, Cornel. "Philosophy and the Afro-American Experience." The Philosophical Forum 9(Winter-Spring 1977-78):117-148.

This essay, originally presented as a paper by Professor West, explores the question: "How does philosophy relate to the Afro-American experience?" West discusses philosophy as formulated by Heidegger, Wittgenstein and Dewey. Each philosopher, he observes, does ccontribute certain techniques toward our understanding of the Afro-American experience. The application of these techniques in analyzing the Afro-American experience is viewed by West as Afro-American philosophy. West further discusses what results can be expected from such a philosophy.

SELECTED DISSERTATIONS

(043B) Boxhill, Bernard R. "A Philosophical Examination of Black Protest Thought." Ph.D. dissertation, University of California,

Los Angeles, 1971.

Focusing on the plight of Black people as described and discussed in the writings of W. E. B. DuBois, Frantz Fanon and five other Black writers, Boxhill attempts to uncover the factual and philosophical presuppositions in these works as well as to judge their admissibility. Four propositions are considered in the discussion. They are: (1) it is the right of Black people to cultivate and preserve their authentic heritage; (2) it is the right of Black people to be separated from white people; (3) revolution by violence is the prerogative of Black people; and (4) the contemporary generation of Blacks is entitled to reparations, because of past wrongs inflicted upon their ancestors by whites.

(044B) Curry, Blanche R. "An Unconventional Theory of Progress." Ph.D. dissertation, Brown University, 1979.

Curry analyzes three major theories of historical change: (1) the cylical theory; (2) the christian theory; and (3) the linear theory. She concludes that each theory is inadequate to explain historical change and advocates a new viable theory of historical change.

(045B) Garrison, George R. "A Critical Appraisal of William James' Moral and Social Philosophy." Ph.D. dissertation, State University of New York at Buffalo, 1976.

The aim of this study is to evaluate the main ideas in the moral and social philosophy of William James. This objective is achieved by: (1) analyzing the epistemic foundation of James' concept of human freedom; (2) examining James' concept of the indeterminate, pluralistic universe and his concept of a finite God; (3) discussing James' moral theory as biological utilitarianism; (4) examining the claim by Ralph Boston Perry that James was a great social and political reformer; and (5) evaluating James' social philosophy.

(046B) Harris, Leonard. "Racism and the Materialist Anthropology of Karl Marx." Ph.D. dissertation, Cornell University, 1974.

Karl Marx's materialistic view of man in the light of racism is analyzed in this work. Harris asserts that Marx erroneously believed that the real interest of the working class represented universal human emancipation. Marx, Harris argues, did not understand the internal dynamics of the material nature of man.

(047B) Hopkins, John Orville. "The Social Ethics of Jacques Maritain and the Justification of Afro-American Education." Ph.D. dissertation, Columbia University, 1976.

Employing the normative, descriptive, and analytic methods of investigation, this study is a work in social ethics. It is an inquiry into the relationship between the social ethics espoused by Jacques Maritain and the failure to create effective social and political policies for the governance of a just contemporary education system for Black Americans in the United States.

(048B) McDade, Jesse. "Frantz Fanon: The Ethical Justification of Revolution." Ph.D. dissertation, Boston University Graduate School, 1971.

Normative justification for revolution as discussed in the writings of Frantz Fanon is presented in this study. The works of Fanon which are analyzed are Black Skins, White Masks; A Dying Colonialism; Toward the African Revolution; and The Wretched of the Earth. McDade concludes that Fanon's model for a normative argument for revolution was developed from Hegel through Marx and used by the Existentialists. Fanon's distinctive contribution, however, was that he adopted the model to contemporary revolutionary politics.

(049B) Murungi, John J. "Two Views of History: A Study of the Relation of European and African Culture." Ph.D. dissertation, Pennsylvania State University, 1970.

Two views of history used to interpret African culture are discussed in this study. They are evolutionary history which is futuristic and was adopted by Europeans during the Colonial era and non-evolutionary history which is African in origin and presents man as having his being in full at all times. Murungi analyzes each view and concludes that Africans must adopt the non-evolutionary view of history to interpret their culture in order to perserve their humanity.

(050B) Outlaw, Lucius T. "Language and the Transformation of Consciousness: Foundations for a Hermeneutic of Black Culture." Ph.D. dissertation, Boston College, 1972.

Black people in the United States and in other countries where they had been colonized have been historically the victims of a duel consciousness. One facet of consciousness was identified with the larger society while the other facet gave expression to African origins. There is evidence that this conflict of duel consciousness is being resolved by many Black people who are developing new meanings in language, speech and other symbolic orders. In this study, Outlaw develops a systematic framework of thought to investigate and properly understand these new contemporary terms of discourse and expression among many Blacks which reflect a new unity of consciousness.

(051B) Simpson, Lorenzo Charles, Jr. Technology and Temporality: A Critique of Instrumental Rationality." Ph.D. dissertation, Yale University, 1978.

Simpson critically analyzes instrumental rationality in this study. He focuses on the consequences which this kind of interpretation of rationality has for the human phenomena of freedom and evaluation. He argues that the consequences are destructive.

(052B) Tolliver, Joseph T. "Reasons Perception, and Information: An Outline of An Information: Theoretic Epistemology." Ph.D. dissertation, The Ohio State University, 1979.

Tolliver develops a theory of perceptual knowledge, of our knowledge of physical objects and their properties. It is based on the assumption that the reasons upon which these beliefs are based must contain information about the states of nature believed in if those beliefs are to be instances of knowledge.

(053B) Washington, Johnny. "Hannah Arendt's Conception of the Political Realm." Ph.D. dissertation, Stanford University, 1978.

Hannah Arendt's views on politics as presented in her book, The Human Condition, and other writings are considered. In his analysis, Washington uses the ideas of Dewey , Kant and Bergson to highlight the concepts advanced by Arendt.

(054B) West, Cornel R. "Ethics, Historicism and the Marxist Tradition." Ph.D. dissertation, Princeton University, 1980.

The historistic approach to ethics, focusing on the Marxist tradition, is examined. West distinguishes between the moderate historic approach and the radical historic approach to ethics. He shows that Marx adopted the radical historic approach, but that three major Marxist philosophers, Engels, Kautsky and Lukacs, used the moderate historistic approach to ethics because they misread Marx's crucial metaphilosophical move in which he became disillusioned with the vision of philosophy as a search for certainty and foundation.

(055B) Williams, Robert C. "A Study of Religious Language: Analysis/ Interpretation of Selected Afro-American Spirituals with Reference to Black Religious Philosophy." Ph.D. dissertation, Columbia University, 1975.

An exposition of the nature and meaning of Afro-American spirituals as an index to Black Folkloric philosophical vision is the subject of this study. Three key observations are made. They are: (1) these spirituals reflect what the slave community felt about daily life and its possibilities; (2) members of the community perceived their lives as related to an ultimate and sacred order of meaning and power; and (3) the language of these songs present insights into the nature of Black religious philosophy.

C.
Black Religion: Faith, Hope and Liberation

BIBLIOGRAPHIES

(001C) The Howard University Bibliography of African and Afro-American Religious Studies. With locations in American Libraries. Compiled by Ethel L. Williams and Clifton Brown. Wilmington, DE.: Scholarly Resources, Inc.,]977.

This is a comprehensive bibliographical guide to more than 13,000 primary and secondary works in African, Afro-Caribbean and Afro-American religious studies located in 230 repositories in the United States. The books, periodical articles and analytics are listed under five major headings: (1) "African Heritage;" (2) "Christianity and Slavery in the New World"; (3) "The Black Man and His Religious Life in the Americas"; (4) "Civil Rights Movement"; and (5) "The Contemporary Scene." In addition to a general index, this work includes a comprehensive appendix of 6,000 autobiographical and biographical works and a guide to unpublished manuscripts.

GENERAL HISTORIES

(002C) *DuBois, W. E. B., ed. The Negro Church: Report of a Social Study Made Under the Direction of Atlanta University; Together with the Proceedings of the Eighth Conference Held at Atlanta University, May 26, 1903. Atlanta, GA.: The Atlanta University Press, 1903.

Included in the Atlanta University Publications (see 030A), this early comprehensive study of the Black church examines many aspects of this institution. The research of several prominent scholars, a host of college students, ministers and religious organizations was utilized to complete this study which covers: (1) the history of the Black church from its African origins through the early years of the twentieth century; (2) missionary enterprises; (3) the Black church in antebellum America; (4) the Black church in 1890; (5) local studies of the Black church in 1902-03; and (6) survey of various Black denominations.

(003C) Fordham, Monroe. Major Themes in Northern Black Religious Thought, 1800-1860. Hicksville, NY: Exposition Press, 1975.

Free Blacks in antebellum America developed a Christian philosophy which would enable them to deal effectively with the oppressive society in which they found themselves. Using the Functional theory, Fordham views Christian theology of the period as addressing the adaptive needs of Black people. Although the adaptive function has been a constant in Black Christian theology, its emphasis has varied as times and circumstances have changed. In examining Black Christian theology in antebellum America, this study attempts to identify what major themes were used to meet the adaptive needs and concerns of free Northern Blacks during these years.

(004C) Frazier, E. Franklin. The Negro Church in America/The Black Church Since Frazier, by C. Eric Lincoln. New York: Schocken Books, 1963, 1974.

Published in one volume, these two classic works discuss the development of organized religion among Afro-Americans. Frazier's study traces the evolution of the Negro church in America from early times through the early 1960s. He does not, as many other scholars have, view the Negro church's beginning as a continuation of African tribal life, but as a Christian religion which gave the transplanted slave a sense of cohesion. C. Eric Lincoln in The Black Church Since Frazier declares "The Negro church that Frazier wrote about no longer exists. It died an agonized death in the harsh turmoil... of the decade of the 'Savage Sixties.' Out of the ashes of its funeral pyre there sprang the bold, strident, self-conscious phoenix that is the contemporary Black church." It is this new Black church which Dr. Lincoln analyzes in his penetrating work.

(005C) *Mays, Benjamin and Nicholson, Joseph. The Negro's Church. New York: Institute of Social and Religious Research, 1933.

Based on the original study of 609 urban and 185 rural churches, this landmark work investigates several features of the Negro church. Among some of them are: the urban and rural ministry; worship activities; the church programs; worship rituals; fellowship and community activities; and the genius of the Negro church.

(006C) Roberts, James Deotis. Roots of a Black Future: Family and Church. Philadelphia: Westminister, 1980.

Roberts presents an enlightening discussion of how historically the African religious background of Afro-Americans has encouraged their vision of the church as the extended family of God. He warns that the Black church has the primary task of strengthening all Black families.

(007C) Simpson, George Eaton. Black Religions in the New World. New York: Columbia University Press, 1978.

In this history of the religions of persons of African descent in the New World, Simpson traces the evolution of these religions in North and South America as well as the Caribbean. The systems of belief and the rituals of each religion are presented and discussed. This wide-ranging work includes historical churches, cults, sects, pentecostals and spiritualists.

(008C) *Woodson, Carter G. The History of the Negro Church. Washington, DC: Associated Publishers, 1921.

This pioneering history of the Black church by Dr. Woodson is a thorough examination of the rise of institutionalized religion among Blacks in America. Beginning with the early efforts of white missionaries to convert the "bondsman," this work traces Black and white involvement in the development of Black religion and the Black church from the late seventeenth century through the early decades of the twentieth century.

DENOMINATIONAL HISTORIES AND COMMENTARIES

The African Methodist Episcopal Church

(009C) *Payne, Daniel A. (bp) History of the African Methodist Episcopal Church. Nashville: A. M. E. Sunday School Union and Publishing House, 1891.

This definitive history of the African Methodist Episcopal Church by one of its most scholarly bishops covers the years from 1784 through 1856. Researched and written over a period of forty-three years, this earliest of Black religious denominational histories is based on original documents and interviews with early denominational church leaders.

(010C Smith, Charles S. A History of the African Methodist Episcopal Church. Vol. 2. Philadelphia: Book Concern of the A. M. E. Church, 1922.

This supplemental volume to Bishop Payne's History of the African Methodist Episcopal Church traces the growth and development of the A. M. E. Church from 1856 through the early 1920s.

The African Methodist Episcopal Zion Church

(011C) Walls, William J. (bp) The African Methodist Espicopal Zion Church: Reality of the Black Church. Charlotte, NC: A. M. E. Zion Publishing House, 1974.

This well-documented history of the African Methodist Episcopal Zion Church by one of its bishops begins with a discussion of the genesis of Black religion in Africa focusing on the Methodist identity. As the narrative unfolds, it shifts to: (1) the establishment of the African Methodist Episcopal Church in the United States under the leadership of James Varick in 1796; and (2) its subsequent growth through the nineteenth and twentieth centuries.

The African Orthodox Church

(012C) Terry-Thompson, Arthur Cornelius. The History of the African Orthodox Church. New York: n. p., 1956?; New York: Beacon Press.

In the early 1920s, Dr. George Alexander McGuire, a West Indian of African descent who was an Episcopal priest and a physician, decided to leave the Episcopal Church and start his own Church. On September 2, 1921, at the Church of the Good Shepherd in New York City, the organization of the African Orthodox Church was consummated, and Dr. McGuire was elected its first Bishop. This work treats briefly the religious history of the denomination of Orthodox Churches from 43 A. D. through the middle 1950s, but focuses on the African Orthodox Church from 1921 discussing its doctrines, rituals and organization.

African Union Methodist Protestant Church
and
Union American Methodist Episcopal Church

(013C) Baldwin, Lewis. Invisible Strands in African Methodism: A History of the African Union Methodist Protestant and Union American Methodist Episcopal Churches. Metuchen, NJ: The American Theological Library Association and Scarecrow Press, 1983.

This historical study is devoted to the development of several regional Black Methodist denominations which grew out of the split with Asbury Methodist Church of Wilmington, Delaware (white) which was led by Peter Spencer and William Anderson, two Black lay preachers, in 1805.

The Baptists

(014C) Jackson, J. H. A Story of Christian Activism: The History of the National Baptist Convention, U. S. A., Inc., Nashville: Townsend Press, 1980.

Researched and written by Dr. Joseph H. Jackson, president of the National Baptist Convention, U. S. A., Inc., 1954-1979, this detailed history traces the development of the Convention from its founding years 1880-1895 to 1979. Dr. Jackson has based his narrative on documents, personal interviews and previous published histories. This is the definitive history of the Black Baptist movement in the United States.

(015C) Jordan, Lewis G. Negro Baptist History, U. S. A., 1750-1930. Nashville: The Sunday School Publishing Board of the National

Baptist Convention, U. S. A., Inc., 1930.

This is a history of the Black Baptist movement written under the auspices of the National Baptist Convention, U.S.A., Inc. Although this work is rather vague on activities of Black Baptists in antebellum America, it does present a thorough account of the development of Black Baptist churches between 1865 and the late 1920s.

(016C) Sobel, Mechal. Trabelin' On: The Slave Journey to An Afro-Baptist Faith. Westport, CT: Greenwood Press, 1979.

Advancing the thesis that the acculturation process of slaves and their progeny resulted in an Afro-Christian worldview, Sobel focuses on the religious aspects of this process. He describes how Afro-Americans, both free and slave, became participants in the white Baptist churches of the South, established their own Baptist churches, and organized an underground Baptist church. This useful study has three appendixes which include statistics and facts on Black Baptist churches between 1758-1864.

(017C) Tyms, James D. The Rise of Religious Education Among Negro Baptists: A Historical Case Study. New York: Exposition Press, 1965.

This comprehensive survey of the religious education activities of Blacks among Baptists covers the years from the last decade of the eighteenth century through the early 1960s. It is divided into five sections: (1) "Social Backgrounds"; (2) "Religious Education Before Emancipation"; (3) "Religious Education of the Middle Period, 1865-1896"; (4) "Religious Education Under Negro Baptist Leadership, 1896-1961"; and (5) "Summary and Conclusions."

The Muslims

(018C) Austin, Allan D. African Muslims in Antebellum America: A Sourcebook. New York: Garland Publishing Co., 1984.

This compilation of the personal narratives of fifteen African Muslims who were brought to the United States during slavery sheds new light on the Afro-American religious Muslim experience prior to the twentieth century. Containing a bibliography and thirty-six photographs, this work includes reproductions of Arabic manuscripts left by these early Muslims.

(019C) Lincoln, Charles Eric. The Black Muslims in America. Revised edition. Boston: Beacon Press, 1973.

This comprehensive study traces the growth of the Black Muslim Movement in America from its Black nationalist roots of the 1930s through 1972 when, as the Nation of Islam, it had become one of the major religious denominations among Black Americans. Dr. Lincoln discusses the probable causes within the American social structure for the development of the Movement as well as examines closely the inner workings and tensions of the Nation of Islam.

(020C) Muhammad, Elijah. Message to the Black Man in America. Chicago: Muhammad's Temple No. 2 Publications Department, 1965.

Elijah Muhammad, Messenger of Allah and Teacher of the So-called Negroes, discusses in this book the tenets of the Nation of Islam as they relate to Black Americans. Outlining in his discussion of the various programs of the Nation of Islam, Muhammad, also, comments on such subjects as: "The Bible and The Holy Qur-an"; "The Persecution of the Righteous"; and "Hypocrites, Disbelievers and Obedience."

The Christian Methodist Episcopal Church

(021C) Harris, E. W. F. and Craig, H. M. Christian Methodist Episcopal Church Through the Years. Rev. ed. Jackson, TN: The C. M. E. Publishing House, 1965.

Supplementing Phillips' The History of the Colored Methodist Church (see 022C), this work records the denomination's history through the early 1960s. Importantly, it discusses the denomination's reasons behind the decision to change its name to the Christian Methodist Episcopal Church.

(022C) Phillips, C. H. The History of the Colored Methodist Episcopal Church of America. Book One and Two. 3rd ed. Jackson, TN: The C. M. E. Publishing House, 1925.

This detailed account of the history of the Colored Methodist Episcopal Church reports on its growth from 1870 through the early 1920s. It focuses on its organization, resulting from its split with the Methodist Episcopal Church, South (white), and its subsequent development into a major Black denomination.

The Church of God In Christ

(023C) Patterson, James O. (bp.), Ross, Germain R., and Atkins, Julia Mason. History and Formative Years of the Church of God In Christ. With excerpts from the Life and Writings of its Founder, Biship C. H. Mason. Memphis: Church of God In Christ Publishing House, 1969.

Recording the history of the Church of God In Christ from 1907 when Elder C. H. Mason, its first bishop, organized it in Memphis to the late 1960s, this work includes a biography of Mason, many of the denomination's doctrines, and brief biographical sketches of its past and present leaders.

Pentecostals

(024C) Paris, Arthur E. Black Pentecostalism: Southern Religion in an Urban World. Amherst: University of Massachusetts Press, 1982.

This important study traces the development of the Pentecostal movement among Blacks from the rural South to the Urban North. Describing Pentecostal churches as very sophisticated institutions, Paris emphasizes the importance of the role of rituals in the lives of their members.

(025C) Williams, Melvin D. Community in A Pentecostal Church: An Anthropological Study. Pittsburgh: University of Pittsburgh Press, 1974.

Based on three years of anthropological observation of the congregation and services of a Pittsburgh Pentecostal church, this study seeks to discuss the quality of the social relations, communal ideology and social group behavior of its members.

CULTS AND SECTS

(026C) Brotz, Howard. The Black Jews of Harlem: Negro Nationalism and the Dilemmas of Negro Leadership. New York: Free Press, 1964.

The Commandment Keepers Congregation of the Living God, Harlem's largest Black Jewish congregation, is the focus of this study. Brotz describes in detail the organization and rituals of this cult and discusses the ethos behind its existence. Presumeably, all Black Americans are Ethiopian Jews or Falashas. Even though Brotz succeeds in presenting a rather complete picture of this Harlem congregation, this study would have been more significant had the Black Jewish congregations in other cities like Chicago been included.

(027C) *Fauset, Arthur Huff. Black Gods of the Metropolis: Negro Religious Cults of the Urban North. Philadelphia: University of Pennsylvania Press, 1944. (Reprint).

In this classic study, which has been used as a model for similar studies, the author analyzes five Black cults in Phildadelphia. They are: Father Devine's Peace Mission Movement; Mount Sinai Holy Church of America; The United House of Prayer for All Peoples; and The Moorish Science Temple of America.

(028C) Washington, Joseph R., Jr. Black Sects and Cults, New York: Doubleday, 1972.

Washington examines in this study the Pentecostals, Sanctified Holiness, Baptists and Methodists sects as well as the followers of Father Devine, Daddy Grace, and the Reverend Albert B. Cleage. He concludes that the great creativity among Blacks in religion is due to the lack of normal outlets in the general society.

BLACK THEOLOGY

(029C) Black Theology II: Essays on the Formation and Outreach of Contemporary Black Theology. Edited by Calvin E. Bruce and William R. Jones. Canbury, NJ: Associated University Presses, 1978.

Written by Black and white, male and female theologians, this collection of eleven essays attempts to further define Black theology and lay a foundation for its future direction beyond the "rage stage." These writers make an effort to reform the formative aspects of Black theology.

(030C) Cleage, Albert B., Jr. The Black Messiah. New York: Sheed and Ward, 1968.

This series of sermons by the pastor of Detroit's Shrine of the Black Madonna Church advances the concept of the Black Messiah. It is based on the assumption that the Israelites who opposed the Romans were Black. The Reverend Cleage urges Black Americans in these sermons to establish their own nation within the United States.

(031C) Cone, James H. A Black Theology of Liberation. Philadelphia: Lippincott, 1970.

Professor Cone presents a systematic treatment of the content of theology and traditional Christian doctrines from the perspective of the struggle for Black liberation. Cone contends that "Christianity is essentially a religion of liberation." Addressed primarily to Blacks, Cone's theology has a universal application "since Blackness symbolizes oppression and liberation in any society."

(032C) Cone, James H. For My People: Black Theology and the Black Church. Maryknoll, NY: Orbis, 1984.

Professor Cone assesses the development of Black theology during the last twenty years in this bold commentary. He suggests that the Black church and Black theology should: (1) discard their history of male privilege; (2) use Marxism as a tool of social criticism; (3) realize the relationship between racism, sexism, and classicism in programs for change; and (4) join the Third World and other minorities to effect change.

(033C) Cone, James H. God of the Oppressed. New York: Seabury, 1975.

In this work Professor Cone bases his Black theology on a three part thesis. They are: (1) "to have any real meaning theology must be existential"; (2) "the freedom of the poor and the oppressed is the core of the Scripture, consequently if Scripture is taken as authoritative, then the Scripture's God and Jesus Christ are meaningless aside from this essential liberation"; and (3) "both God and Jesus have immersed themselves in and can only be found in the Black experience."

(034C) Jones, Major J. Black Awareness: A Theology of Hope. Nashville: Abingdon, 1971.

Placing the Black Experience in historical perspective, Professor Jones discusses the pre- and post-civil war expressions of the white and Black churches to this Experience. Analyzing the nature of the Church in terms of the Black perspective, Jones interprets the meaning of current Black awareness. Against this backdrop, Jones presents what he envisions as the implications of a Theology of Hope for the Black Community. In his introduction, Jones makes the following assessment:

> "More perhaps than any other, this theology of hope seeks to be a this-world interpretation; and, in this light, it seeks to look at the hope of a people from an internalized black awareness frame of reference. Though it is centered in black awareness, such a hope is under God; it is a hope seen from a 'black perspective."

(035C) Jones, Major J. Christian Ethics for Black Theology. Nashville, TN: Abingdon, 1974.

Professor Jones sets forth in this work suggestions for building new Black/white relations through Black theology. He writes:

> "...the book takes the general position that the new Testament concept of reconciliation is not the relationship that is now being sought by black and white people in America; that is for the simple reason that the two races have never had an ideal reconciliation. Rather the book seeks to suggest ethical formulations necessary to build a totally new creative relationship that has never heretofore existed between black and white people in America."

(036C) King, Martin Luther, Jr. Why We Can't Wait. New York: New American Library, 1963.

In this work, Dr. Martin Luther King, Jr. lays the groundwork for the development of Black theology. Written in the wake of the Birmingham demonstrations, it sets forth the basic tenets of Black theology: a theology which will liberate Black people through the practice of Christian virtues.

(037C) Leckey, Robert S. and Wright, H. Elliott, eds. Black Manifesto: Religion, Racism and Reparations. New York: Sheed and Ward, 1969.

The Black Manifesto, which grew out of the National Black Economic Development Conference that was held in Detroit in

April 1969, is a mix of racism, religion and reparations. "Our Fight," it proclaims, "is against racism, captialism and imperialism and we are dedicated to building a socialistic society in the United States."

(038C) *Mays, Benjamin Elijah. The Negro's God as Reflected in His Literature. Boston: Chapman and Grimes, 1938.

In this classic work, Dr. Mays analyzes the concept of God as represented in the literature by Black authors in works published from 1760 through 1937. He examines: "Classical literature," slave narratives, autobiographies, biographies, addresses, novels, poetry, and social commentaries; as well as "Mass literature," which includes prayers, sermons and spirituals.

(039C) Roberts, James Deotis. A Black Political Theology. Philadelphia: Westminister, 1974.

Drawing on the Black American and African religious experience, current relevant theology of Protestantism and the contemporary Latin American theologies of liberation, Professor Roberts develops a viable experientially-based Black theology.

(040C) Smith, Archie, Jr. The Relational Self Ethics and Therapy From A Black Church Perspective. Nashville: Abingdon, 1982.

The author develops a new framework for Black liberation ministry in this study. It is based on the concept of relational self and christian social ethics.

(041C) Washington, Joseph R., Jr. Black Religion and Christianity in the United States. Boston: Beacon Press, 1964.

In the four essays included in this work, Washington argues that American Black churches are not Christian, but have focused on "freedom-rights opportunity." This focus Washington identifies as the real Black religion with social protest as its main thrust. Consequently, he suggests that white churches can make a positive contribution to Blacks by accepting them into their churches and into the mainstream of religion of America.

(042C) Wilmore, Gayraud S. and Cone, James H., eds. Black Theology: A Documentary History, 1966-1979. New York: Orbis Books, 1979.

Edited by two prominent Black theologians, this volume includes documents, essays, articles and commentaries by Black and white writers that: (1) document the origins and the development of Black theology; (2) discuss the programs of Black theology; and (3) examine various aspects of the subject. This comprehensive work is divided into three sections: "Part I: The End of An Era: Civil Rights to Black Power; Part II: The Attack on White Religion; Part III: Black Theology and the Response of White Theologians." An extensive bibliography on

Black theology, by V. T. Eason is included.

(043C) West, Cornel. <u>Prophesy Deliverance! An Afro-American Revolutionary Christianity</u>. Philadelphia: Westminister Press, 1982.

In this provocative work, Professor West proposes an alliance between traditional Afro-American Christian religion and the progressive Marxism espoused by Rosa Luxemburg as a basis for the formation of a revolutionary Afro-American Christian philosophy.

SIGNIFICANT BIOGRAPHICAL AND AUTOBIOGRAPHICAL WORKS

(044C) Ansbro, John J. <u>Martin Luther King, Jr.: The Making of a Mind</u>. Maryknoll, NY: Orbis Books, 1982.

In this perceptive biography, Ansbro analyzes the intellectual development of Martin Luther King, Jr. as a student, theologian and civil rights leader. Through interviews with faculty members who taught King at Morehouse College, Crozier Theological Seminary and Boston University, Ansbro gathered data which he used to track King's growth as a student. He discusses the influence on King of such philosophers as Hegel, Kierkegaard, Thoreau and Rauschenbusch in his somewhat successful attempt to define the intellectual base from which King developed his non-violent ethic.

(045C) Burkett, Randall K. and Newman, Richard, eds. <u>Black Apostles: Afro-American Clergy Confront the Twentieth Century</u>. Boston: G. K. Hall, 1978.

Fifteen Black Religious leaders of the nineteenth and twentieth centuries are discussed by various writers in this anthology of articles. These leaders are: Alexander Bedward; Edward W. Blyden; Father Divine; Arnold J. Ford; Francis J. Grimke; Gordon Blaine Hancock; George Edmund Haynes; James Theodore Holly; Harold M. Kingsley; Patriarch McGuire; Reverdy C. Ransom; William J. Seymour; Henry McNeal Turner; Alexander Walters; and George Washington Woodbey.

(046C) Burnham, Kenneth E. <u>God Comes to America: Father Divine and the Peace Mission Movement</u>. Boston: Lambeth Press, 1979.

Based on what appears to be a critical examination of materials of the Peace Mission Movement, Burnham discusses perceptively its internal organizational machinations and principles. Father Divine's development as a charismatic leader is scrutinized in this work which focuses on his theology with emphasis on Divine's economic message to his followers.

(047C) George, Carol V. R. <u>Segregated Sabbaths: Richard Allen and the Rise of Independent Black Churches, 1760-1840</u>. New York: Oxford University Press, 1973.

Richard Allen, the first Bishop of the African Methodist Episcopal Church, was, unquestionably, the most powerful Black man in America during the early decades of the nineteenth century. Carol V. R. George closely examines Allen's influence on the establishment of independent Black churches of all denominations between 1790 and 1840. After presenting a sketch of Allen's early life, George discusses his role in the founding of the A. M. E. Church, his influence in the organizing of other Black churches and his participation as a leader of the first Negro National Convention in 1831.

(048C) Jackson, Rebecca. Gifts of Power: The Writings of Rebecca Jackson, Black Visionary, Shaker Eldress. Ed. by Jean McMahon Humez. Amherst, MA: University of Massachusetts Press, 1981.

Rebecca Cox Jackson, 1795-1891, was a Black visionary and founder of a Shaker community in Philadelphia. This compilation of her writings documents the spiritual growth of one of the most remarkable Black women religious leaders of the nineteenth century.

(049C) Little, Malcolm. The Autobiography of Malcolm X, by Malcolm X with Alex Haley. New York: Grove, 1965.

Born Malcolm Little in 1922 in Omaha, the man who became Malcolm X was a pimp, hustler, drug addict and a prison inmate before he redeemed his humanity through introspective soul wrenching. With the aid of Alex Haley, Malcolm X recounts with candor in this narrative his odyssey from early childhood to his years as the articulate spokesman for the Nation of Islam and many Black Americans.

(050C) Mays, Benjamin E. Born to Rebel: An Autobiography. New York: Scribner, 1971.

In this memoir, Dr. Mays not only chronicles his life from his early years in South Carolina in the 1890s through his presidency at Atlanta's Morehouse College, but he gives an intimate and authoritative view of race relations in the United States during the first seven decades of the twentieth century. Dr. Mays personal victories and losses with injustices, both racial and non-racial, encountered in his life time are retold to give an indepth portrait of the distinguished educator, race relations spokesman, theologian and arbitrator.

(051C) Paris, Peter J. Black Leaders in Conflict: Joseph H. Jackson, Martin Luther King, Jr., Malcolm X, Adam Clayton Powell, Jr. New York: Pilgrim Press, 1978.

In this excellent analysis, Paris presents the conflicting views on race relations of four major Black religious leaders. Their personal philosophies on such issues as federal legislation, boycotts, civil disobedience, Black Power, and morality in America differ. Paris suggests that their views are more complimentary than mutually exclusive and calls for a coalition of attitudes among the four leaders which could produce cooperative action.

(052C) Payne, Daniel (bp.). Reflections of Seventy Years. Nashville, A. M. E. Sunday School Union and Publishing House, 1888.

This personal memoir is undoubtedly one of the most important to flow from the pen of a nineteenth century religious leader. In it, Bishop Payne of the A. M. E. Church recaptures with great discernment his life from 1811 in antebellum Charleston, South Carolina through the late 1880s. In this lucid narrative, Payne's exceptional life unfolds as he recollects his years as a brilliant young teacher in Charleston before the Civil War, his eventful rise in the A. M. E. Church, his presidency of Wilberforce University and his final years as a world church leader.

(053C) Powell, Adam Clayton, Jr. Adam by Adam. New York: Dial Press, 1971.

Adam Clayton Powell, Jr., as pastor of New York's huge and historic Abyssinion Baptist Church and twenty-five years a congressman, was a national religious and political leader. In this autobiographical narrative, Powell discusses his personal life, his fight for civil rights legislation, his ministry, and his troubles with the federal government.

(054C) Reynolds, Barbara A. Jesse Jackson: The Man, The Movement, and The Myth. Chicago: Nelson Hall, 1975.

Written by a Chicago newspaper reporter, this well-researched biography presents a stark appraisal of one of America's most charismatic religious leaders. Focusing primarily on Reverend Jackson's activities as leader of Chicago-based SCLC Operation Breadbasket and later his own Operation PUSH, Reynolds unearths many little-known facts and circumstances surrounding the religious, political and civil rights episodes in the life of the Reverend Jesse Jackson.

(055C) Thurman, Howard. With Head and Heart: The Autobiography of Howard Thurman. New York: Harcourt Brace Jovanovich, 1979.

In lucid prose, Howard Thurman reviews the major events in his productive life. Highly analytical, this personal memoir recounts Thurman's years of training at Morehouse College and Rochester-Colgate, his fledgling years as a minister and theologian, and the challenging experiences which vaulted him into national renown as a educator, theologian and minister.

(056C) Walters, Alexander (bp.). My Life and Work. New York: Fleming Revell, 1917.

The twenty-fourth bishop of the A. M. E. Zion Church, a pioneer Pan Africanist and a world ecumenical leader, Bishop Alexander Walters was one of the most renowed Black religious leaders in the early years of the twentieth century. In this autobiography, written in the last year of his life, Bishop

Walters describes his extraordinary life and career. As a document providing an intimate view of race relations in the United States in the late nineteenth century and the Pan African movement in the early years of the twentieth century, it is invaluable.

(057C) Webb, Lillian Ashcraft. About My Father's Business: The Life of Elder Micheaux. Westport, CT: Greenwood Press,]98].

This biography of Elder Lightfoot Solomon Micheaux, the radio evangelist who was popular in Washington, D. C. in the 1930s and 1940s, is a first rate analysis of his career and his Church of God and Gospel Spreading Association.

(058C) Weisbrot, Robert. Father Divine and the Struggle for Racial Equality. Urbana: University of Illinois Press, 1983.

Focusing on the Depression years, this study, assesses Father Divine and his Peace Mission as agents of social change striving for social betterment of Black as well as white Americans. Viewing Father Divine as an important reformer, Wiesbrot discusses the Peace Mission's economic, altruistic, political and social activities and Father Divine's influence on the Roosevelt Administration's civil rights policies.

(059C) Williams, Ethel L. Biographical Directory of Negro Ministers. 2nd ed. Metuchen, NJ: Scarecrow Press, 1970.

This biographical source contains concise biographical sketches on living Black American clergy in all religious denominations. Arranged alphabetically by biographee, this directory has a geographical index which is accessed by state and city.

(060C) Young, Henry J. Major Black Religious Leaders Since 1940. Nashville: Abingdon Press, 1979.

Beginning with W. E. B. Dubois and ending with James H. Cone, this collective biography discusses the lives and theology of fourteen Black national religious and secular leaders. Young analyzes in these biographical essays the evolution of Black religious thought from accommodationism through Black liberation theology.

Outstanding Sermons and Pastoral Commentaries

(061C) King, Martin Luther, Jr. Strength To Love. New York: Harper Row, 1963.

In these seventeen sermons, Dr. King eloquently presents his theology of love. Published at the height of civil rights demonstrations in the South, many of these sermons were conceived and written by Dr. King while he was in Southern jails.

(062C) King, Martin Luther, Jr. Where Do We Go From Here. New York: Harper & Row, 1967.

Dr. King rejects in this commentary the Black Power Movement as an impediment to the Civil Rights Movement. Instead he suggests that a political coalition between Blacks and whites should be developed to resolve the race problem.

(063C) Powell, Adam Clayton. Keep the Faith, Baby. New York: Trident Press, 1967.

This collection of sermons delivered by the Reverend Adam Clayton Powell, Jr. at his Abyssinian Baptist Church illustrates his ability to relate Scripture to every day problems. These sermons cover such subjects as civil rights, Black Power, McCarthyism, and God Is Dead.

(064C) Thurman, Howard. The Luminous Darkness: A Personal Interpretation of the Anatomy of Segregation and the Ground of Hope. New York: Harper, 1965.

Thurman presents an insightful analysis of America's race problem. Both Black and white, he asserts, are being spiritually harmed by it. When integration is finally realized, he concludes, many wounds on both sides will be apparent. The Church, Thurman says, will be responsible for healing these wounds.

(065C) Thurman, Howard. The Search for Common Ground: An Inquiry Into the Basic of Man's Experiences of Community. New York: Harper, Row, 1971.

Thurman advances the thesis that all life works toward wholeness. He sympathizes with the Black or white individual who believes in separateness. As a Black leader, he outlines a philosophic basis for Black and white coming together.

SELECTED ARTICLES

(066C) Evans, James H. "Toward An Afro-American Theology." Journal of Religious Thought. 40(Fall-Winter 1983-84):39-54.

The author concludes in this overview of Afro-American theology: "All Afro-American theology has as its center God's liberating activity in Jesus Christ in behalf of the depressed. In this sense 'the Lord our God is One."

(067C) Jenkins, J. Dallas. "The Black Agenda for the Eighties." A. M. E. Zion Quarterly Review. 92(January 1981):52-57.

The Secretary of the Department of Evangelism of the African Methodist Episcopal Zion Church makes several predictions about the course of the Black church in the 1980s. Among them are the development of a Black theology and the emergence of credible Black theologians comparable to Tillich, Bultman or Barth. He does not, however, make any substantive observations about priorities for the Black church in the 1980s.

(068C) Lincoln, C. E.: Mamiya, L. H. "Daddy Jones and Father Divine: The Cult As Political Religion," Religion in Life 49(Spring 1980):6-23.

Two prominent religious scholars compare and contrast the political religious aspects of Father Divine's Peace Mission Movement and Jim Jones' People's Temple. Both movements sprang into existence in times of despair: The Peace Mission during the Depression; and The People's Temple in the agony of the 1960s. Jones was a great admirer of Father Divine and attempted, unsuccessfully, to follow in his footsteps as a charismatic leader of a cult.

(069C) Lloyd, Anthony. "Dr. Carl Jung's Concept of Individuation As A Healing Model From The Black Perspective." A. M. E. Zion Quarterly 95(October 1983):37-49.

Lloyd presents an analysis of Jung's Concept of Individuation. Using this concept, he successfully develops a healing model which incorporates the Black experience.

(070C) Mamiya, L. H. "From Black Muslin to Bilalian: The Evolution of A Movement." Journal for the Scientific Study of Religion.

Based on extensive interviews, this study discusses the changes which have occurred in the Black Muslim Movement since the death of Elijah Muhammad. The American Muslim Mission headed by Wallace Muhammad is assessed as a middle class movement while, in contrast, the ressurected Nation of Islam led by Louis Farrakhan is seen as a lower class movement adhering very closely to the doctrines advocated by Elijah Muhammad.

(071C) Mitchell, M. G. "Black Woman's View of Human Liberation." Theology Today. 39(January 1983):421-5.

Mitchell interprets the findings of a study which was conducted on twenty-eight Black women in the ministry. The study was to determine what each respondent: (1) thought of themselves and their ministry; and (2) believe to be her liberation and theology profile. There was a wide variation among the respondents.

(072C) Morrison, Roy D. "The Emergence of Black Theology in America (Harlem Renaissance)." A. M. E. Zion Quarterly 94(October 1982):2-17.

Morrison examines some of the historical, cultural and religious roots of Black theology as well as its major advocates, themes and characteristics. Commenting on the significance of Black theology as a cultural phenomenon, he contends that it developed as a reaction by Black Americans to the failure of classical Christianity to effectively resolve the injustices resulting from the poor state of race relations in the United States.

(073C) Murray, Pauli. "Black, Feminist Theologies: Links, Parallels & Tensions." Christianity & Crisis 40(April 14, 1980):86-95.

Pauli Marshall has distinguished herself as a novelist/short story writer, lawyer, civil rights activist, feminist and currently is an ordanined Episcopal priest. In this perceptive essay, she compares the relationships, common perspectives, points of tension and potential of Black and Feminist theologies as forces for liberation. (An excellent comparative analysis of Black and Feminist theologies.)

(074C) "New Directions in Black Religious Thought (Thematic Issue)," Ed. by Charles Rooks. The Chicago Theological Seminary Register 73(Winter 1983):1-54.

This entire number of The C. T. S. Register is devoted to lectures presented on "Contemporary Horizons in Black Theology" by prominent Black theologians at the Chicago Theological Seminary. The Series of lectures included: "Black Theology and Third World Theologies," by James H. Cone; "Freedom, Otherness, and Religion: Theologies Opaque," by Charles H. Long; "Reinterpretation in Black Church History," by Gayraud S. Wilmore; "Liberation Strategies in Black Theology: Mao, Martin, or Malcolm," by William R. Jones; and "The Future of the Black Church," by Charles S. Spivey. (One of the best contemporary comprehensive forums on Black theology).

(075C) Roberts, J. D. "Ecumenical Concerns Among National Baptists." Journal of Ecumenical Studies. 17(Spring 1980):38-48.

This presentation of the ecumenical activities among Black Baptists traces these efforts from the late nineteenth century through the late 1970s. It considers relations between the independent Black Baptist churches and white churches during the Revolutionary and Antebellum periods; the Black Baptist conventions and national and international groups during the late nineteenth and early twentieth centuries; and contemporary ecumencial concerns and activities of Black Baptists.

(076C) Stewart, Carolyn Fielding, III. "The Method of Correlation in the Theology of James H. Cone." The Journal of Religious Thought. 40(Fall-Winter 1983-84):27-38.

In this analysis of Cone's method of correlation, Steward draws several comparisons between Cone's theology and that of Paul Tillich.

(077C) Usher, Mauricio. "Redemption and the Rise of the Black Church." Perkins School of Theology Journal. 36(Winter 1983): 26-34.

In this illuminating article, Black salvation and the rise of the Black Church are considered. Out of the dehumanizing experiences of slavery, Usher argues, the slaves' hope of deliverance and the concept of Black religious redemption arose which formed the basis for the Black Church in America.

DISSERTATIONS

(078C) Beck, Carolyn Stickney. "Our Own Vine and Fig Tree: The Persistence of An Historical Afro-American Community." Ph.D. dissertation, Bryn Mawr College, 1981.

Based on participant observation and the examination of archives and census records, this is an ethnographic study of Mother Bethel African Methodist Episcopal Church in Philadelphia. It focuses on ethnicity and cultural persistence and utilizes concepts developed by Fredrik Barth, Edward Spicer and Abner Cohen in examining Mother Bethel and its congregation.

(079C) Bynum, La Taunya Marie. "Black Feminist Theology: A New Word About God." D. Min., School of Theology at Claremont, 1980.

Black theology and Feminist theology, Bynum asserts, challenge the assumptions of white and male-dominated theology. There has, however, been a dialogue between Black theology and Feminist theology. Nonetheless, both theologies have not effectively included the Black woman. In an effort to resolve this exclusiveness, an attempt is made in this study to develop a theology which is a synthesis of Black theology and Feminist theology which gives expression to the humanity of the Black woman.

(080C) Evans, Anthony Tyrone. "A Biblical Critique of Selected Issues in Black Theology." Ph.D. dissertation, Dallas Theological Seminary, 1982.

This study discusses Black theology's system of belief in such areas as bibliology, Christology, ecclesiology, and eschatology as advocated by Black theology chief exponents. Evans successfully analyzes and evaluates Black theology to ascertain its compatibility with the Scriptures.

(081C) Franklin, Marion Joseph. "The Relationship of Black Preaching to Black Gospel Music." Ph.D. dissertation, Drew University, 1982.

The objective of this study is to describe the relationship between Black preaching and Black gospel music in the worship service. Providing a model for the teaching of Black gospel music, it, also, discusses such aspects as common meter, short meter, hymns, lining of hymns, the prayer phase and moaning.

(082C) Grayson, John Turner. "Frederick Douglass' Intellectual Development: His Concepts of God, Man and Nature in the Light of American and European Influences." Ph.D. dissertation, Columbia University, 1981.

Based on the assumption that Frederick Douglass intellectual and religious development was discursive, this study advances the thesis that it began while he was still a slave and reached its greatest fulfillment in the last year of his life. This intellectual biography of Douglass' is significant because: (1) he is identified as a major figure who applied Western intellectual and religious ideas to the Black American experience; and (2) he was an eclectic philosopher whose choice of ideas were influenced by his comittment to the freedom of humanity.

(083C) Harris, Michael W. "The Advent of Gospel Blues in Black Old-Line Churches in Chicago, 1932-33 as seen Through the Life and Mind of Thomas Andrew Dorsey." Ph.D. dissertation, Harvard University, 1982.

Until the early 1930s, old-line churches in Chicago developed a liturgy reflective of white middle class churches. Their choirs performed religious music in the tradition of western European choral music. In 1932, at Chicago's Ebenezer Baptist Church, Gospel blues made its debut and spread to other churches in the city. Harris explores the development of Gospel music in Chicago in these early years through the life of Thomas Andrew Dorsey, the father of Gospel music.

(084C) Johnson, Lillie Molliene. "Black American Missionaries in Colonia Africa, 1900-1940: A Study in Government Relations." Ph.D. dissertation, University of Chicago, 1981.

One of the significant issues arising in Colonial Africa was the relationship between colonial governments and missionaries, especially Black American missionaries. This study defines and analyzes the role of Black American missionaries in Colonial Africa. It discusses: (1) the religious and personal histories of Black American individuals and institutions involved in African missionary work; (2) the conflicts which arose between colonial governments and Black American missionaries; and (3) the fears of colonial administrators that Black American missionaries might create centers of discontent among the native Africans.

(085C) Martin, Sandy Dwayne. "The Growth of Christian Missionary Baptist Interest in West Africa Among Southeastern Black Baptists, 1880-1915." Ph.D. dissertation, Columbia University, 1981.

Focusing on the Black Baptist missionary movement in West Africa, this study describes the role played by Black Baptist churches and state conventions in Virginia, North Carolina, South Carolina, Georgia, Florida, Alabama and Tennessee from 1880 through 1915. It investigates the activities of the Baptist Foreign Missionary Mission Convention, 1895-; and the Lott Carey Baptist Foreign Mission Convention, which was organized in 1897.

(086C) Monroe, Johnnie A. "A Descriptive Study of the Origin and Impact of Black Presbyterians United Upon the Mission and Ministry of the Presbytery of Philadelphia." D. Min., Eastern Baptist Theological Seminary, 1980.

Historically, this study contends, Blacks in the United Presbyterian Church, U. S. A. have been excluded from decision and policy making positions. In 1967 Black Presbyterians United was established in Philadelphia "for love and power, and to put a stop to the dehumanizing relationship existing under the aegis of the Church of Jesus Christ." Employing the historical and questionnaire method, Monroe presents a description of the impact of Black Presbyterians United on the "mission and ministry of the Presbytery of Philadelphia."

(087C) Morris, Calvin S. "Reverdy C. Ransom: A Pioneer Black Social Gospeler." Ph.D. dissertation, Boston University, 1982.

Presenting an in-depth examination of activities of a major leader of the African Methodist Episcopal Church during the Progressive Era, this study centers on strategies Ransom used to enact his Social Gospel philosophy in his several pastorates from 1886 to 1912.

(088C) Peck, Gary Richard. "Black Radical Consciousness and the Black Christian Experience: Towards a Critical Sociology of Afro-American Religion." Ph.D. dissertation, University of North Carolina at Chapel Hill, 1983.

After determining the shortcomings of current sociological literature in examining the influences of religion on Black radical consciousness, Peck develops a unique histography to achieve this objective. Using this histography and one designed for youth in Chicago, he attempts to analyze how religious adherences have contributed to Black radical consciousness.

(089C) Trulear, Harold Dean. "An Analysis of the Formative Roles in the Development of Afro-American Religion." Ph.D. dissertation, Drew University, 1983.

Arguing that social structure has been the primary causative factor in the development of Afro-American religion, this researcher points out that previous socio-scientific analysis of the Black church has been skewed in the direction of sociological determinism. This study, however, focuses on the development of the philosophical paradigm which undergirds the sociology of the Black church.

(090C) Williams, Walter L. "Black Americans and the Evangelization of Africa, 1877-1900." Madison, University of Wisconsin, 1982.

This pioneering study of Black American missionaries in Africa is based on primary sources and denominational newspaper articles. Williams advances the thesis that Black American missionaries were instrumental in laying the groundwork for

Pan Africanism. In the appendix is valuable information relative to the records of Black American missionaries and African students.

D.
" . . . To Plead Our Own Cause:" Blacks in Journalism

BIBLIOGRAPHY

(001D) Hill, George H., Comp. 155 Years of Black Media: A Selected Annotated Bibliography. Boston: G. K. Hall, 1984.

Undoubtedly, the most comprehensive work of its kind to appear to date on Blacks in mass communications, this bibliography covers all media where there has been Black involvement. It includes citations to works about Black-owned and Black-oriented media, excluding motion pictures, in newspaper journalism, book publishing, magazine journalism, radio and television journalism, public relations, advertising and communications organizations.

(002D) La Brie, Henry G., III. The Black Press: A Bibliography. 3rd ed., Kennebunkport, Maine: Mercer House Press, 1980.

Including over 400 citations to books, periodical articles, unpublished works and newspaper articles, this work covers Black newspaper and magazine journalism from 1829 through the late 1970s. The citations, however, are not annotated.

(003D) Pride, Amistead S., Comp. 'The Black Press: A Bibliography." Prepared for the Association for Education in Journalism, Ad Hoc Committee on Minority Education. [Jefferson City, Mo., 1968]

Compiled by one of the leading scholars of the Black press as well as a distinguished journalism educator, this classic bibliography contains 386 citations to books, periodical articles, and unpublished works which appeared between 1891 and 1967. It is divided into seven sections: (1) "Advertising and Marketing"; (2) "Analysis and Criticism"; (3) "Biography and History"; (4) "Competition: Coverage of Black Community by Non-Black Media"; (5) "Employment"; (6) "Magazines"; (7) "Radio and Television."

Indexes, Guides and Union Lists

(004D) Black Periodicals and Newspapers: A Union List of Holdings in Libraries of the University of Wisconsin and the Library of the State Historical Society of Wisconsin. Second edition, revised. Compiled by Neil E. Strache, Maureen E. Hady, James P. Danky, Susan Bryl, and Erwin K. Welsch, Madison: State Historical Society of Wisconsin, 1979.

The libraries of the University of Wisconsin and the State Historical Society of Wisconsin have strong collections of Afro-Americana. This union list cites more than 600 Black periodical and newspaper titles housed in these libraries as of February 1979. Included are older titles which have ceased publication as well as current titles. Arranged alphabetically by title, each entry cites the place of publication, publication dates, and library location. The entire list has a subject and geographic index.

(005D) Campbell, Georgetta M. Extant Collections of Early Black Newspapers: A Research Guide to the Black Press, 1880-1915 with an Index to the Boston Guardian. 1902-1904. Troy, N.Y.: Wheston, 1981.

This work is a guide to 233 extant Black newspapers which were published in the United States between 1880 and 1915. In one section, arranged by state, all the extant newspapers published in a state during the period are cited with the names of the repositories where they are held. A second major section is a subject index to extant issues of the Boston Guardian which were published between 1902 and 1904.

(006D) Jacobs, Donald M. ed. Antebellum Black Newspapers: Indices to New York's "Freedom's Journal" (1827-1829); "The Rights of All" (1829); "The Weekly Advocate" (1837); and "The Colored American" (1837-1841). Assisted by Heath Paley, Susan Parker and Diana Silverman. Westport, Conn.: Greenwood Press, 1976.

Containing indices to four early Black newspapers which were published in New York City before the Civil War, this work provides the researcher with ready access to the editorials, letters, news articles and advertisements in these pioneering newspapers in Black journalism. Arranged alphabetically by subject, each entry has references to the date, year, page and column where the item is located. Profiles of the four papers appear before each index.

(007D) La Brie, Henry G., III. A Survey of Black Newspapers in America Rev. ed. Kennebunkport, ME.: Mercer House Press, 1979.

This helpful guide lists all Black newspapers published in the late 1970s. It is arranged alphabetically by state. Each entry contains such items as: owner-publisher; chief executive officer; frequency of publication; and circulation.

(008D) North Carolina Central University. School of Library Science. African-American Materials Project. Newspapers and Periodicals By and About Black People: Southeastern Library Holdings. Compiled by the African-American Materials Project Staff. Assisted by Lillie Dailey Caster. Boston: G. K. Hall, 1978.

One thousand serial titles by and about Blacks in 183 cooperating public, academic and special libraries in Alabama, Georgia, North Carolina, South Carolina, Tennessee and Virginia are reported in this valuable union list. These serial titles include periodicals, newspapers and organizational publications originating in Africa, the West Indies, Mexico, Haiti, Belgium, France, India, Spain, the Netherlands, Great Britain and the United States. Serials cited, which were published in the United States, were issued from Black as well as white presses.

Treatises, Histories and Commentaries

(009D) The Black American and the Press. Edited by Jack Lyle. Los Angeles, CA: The Ward-Ritchie Press, 1968.

In 1967 the University of California at Los Angeles' Foreign Journalism Awards Program held a symposium on the treatment of Black Americans by the press. These proceedings of the symposium include papers discussing different aspects of press coverage of Black Americans by seventeen Black and white journalists and scholars. Among some of the presenters were Armistead Pride, Ralph McGill, Gunnar Myrdal, and Hodding Carter, III.

(010D) Detweiler, Frederick G. Negro Press in the United States. Chicago: University of Chicago Press, 1922.

Published in 1922, this classic work was the first systematic study of the Black press. It analyzes the character of Black newspaper and journals, their editorial content, circulation, and influence on Black and white readers.

(011D) Finkle, Lee. Forum for Protest: The Black Press During World War II. Rutherford, NJ: Associated University Presses, 1975.

During World War II, Black Americans, frustrated in their efforts to gain equality, were generally apathetic toward the war. However, the Black Press, always supportive of patriotism, urged its Black readership to adopt the "Double V" philosophy which advocated victory abroad against the country's enemies and victory at home for the equality of Black Americans. Based on news disseminated by the Black press during World War II, this work analyzes the news content, editorials and columists which were published in 210 Black newspapers between 1941 and 1945. The author declares: "This study evaluates the use of militant rhetoric by a conservative press in trying to channel the activities of an oppressed minority into seeking change within the existing institutions."

(012D) La Brie, Henry G., III. ed. Perspectives of the Black Press,

1974. Kennebunkport, Maine: Mercer House, 1975.

This variegated collection of 18 essays and well-researched articles by leading Black and white scholars, practicioners and educators of Black journalism discuss unique aspects of the Black press and present rare insights into its history, philosophy and functions. Among some of its notable contributions are: "Fifty-five years with the Black Press," by William O. Walker, Publisher, The Cleveland Call and Post Group; "The News That Was," by Dr. Armistead S. Pride, former Head, Department of Journalism, Lincoln University; "The Black Press and Pressure Groups," by Thelma Thurston Gorham, Professor of Journalism, Florida A. & M. University; "Loneliness in the Capital: The Black National Correspondent," by Ethel L. Payne, former Washington Correspondent for Sengstacke Publications; and "The Black Press: A Democratic Society's Catalytic Agent for Building Tomorrow's America," by Dr. Carlton B. Goodlet, Publisher, San Francisco Sun Reporter.

(013D) Penn, I. Garland. The Afro-American Press, and Its Editors. Springfield, Mass.: Wiley & Co., 1891.

This classic work was the earliest study done on the Black press in the United States. Part I contains profiles of all the Black newspapers and magazines which were published in the United States from 1827 to 1891. Part II is devoted to biographical sketches of Black journalists and commentaries on the status and mission of the Black press.

(014D) Suggs, Henry Lewis, ed. The Black Press in the South, 1865-1979. Westport, CT: Greenwood Press, 1983.

This is the first comprehensive study of the Black press in the South. It is composed of twelve substantive articles by historians and specialists of the Southern Black press. Each article is devoted to the development of the Black press in one of the twelve southern states between 1865 and 1879.

(015D) Tinney, James S.; Rectos, Justine J., eds. Issues and Trends in Afro-American Journalism. Lanham, Md.: University Press of America, 1980.

Part one of this collection of essays is devoted to the Black press. A wide range of topics are covered by ten writers such as W. E. B. DuBois and readership studies of Black newspapers. Part two contains fifteen essays on Black broadcasting.

(016D) Wolseley, Roland E. The Black Press, U.S.A. With an introduction by Robert E. Johnson, Executive Director, Jet. Ames, IA: The Iowa State University Press, 1971.

Several areas of the Black press are discussed in this general history and commentary on Black journalism. In three chapters a rather cursory history of the Black press from 1827 to the mid-1960s is presented. The remaining chapters are devoted to: (1) examining the status and operations of current Black newspapers and magazines; and (2) discussing such subjects as the Black journalist today, problems of Black publishers, and Black philosophies of journalism. Wolseley concludes with a perceptive commentary on the future of the Black press.

Biographical Works

(017D) Buni, Andrew. Robert L. Vann of the "Pittsburgh Courier:" Politics and Black Journalism. Pittsburgh: University of Pittsburgh Press, 1974.

Trained as a lawyer, Robert L. Vann served as the first counsel for the new Pittsburgh Courier when it was established in 1910. From that year through 1940, when he died, Vann built the Pittsburgh Courier into one of the major Black newspapers in the United States. In this biography Andrew Buni perceptively assesses Vann's triumphs and failures as publisher, journalist, lawyer and politician.

(018D) Fox, Stephen R. The Guardian of Boston: William Monroe Trotter. New York: Atheneum, 1970.

Along with Booker T. Washington and W. E. B. DuBois, William Monroe Trotter was one of the leading spokesmen for Black America at the turn of the century. In 1901 he founded The Boston Guardian which quickly became the most effective opposition newspaper against Washington's policies. Stephen Fox has written a superior biography on this militant, uncompromising journalist and advocate for Black racial equality in the early years of the twentieth century.

(019D) Hogan, Lawrence D. A Black National News Service: The Associated Negro Press and Claude Barnett, 1919-1945. Rutherford, NJ: Fairleigh Dickinson University Press, 1984.

In 1917 Claude Barnett established the Associated Negro Press (ANP) in Chicago. This quality reporting news service gave Afro-American newspapers comprehensive coverage of personalities, events and institutions in Afro-American life on a national basis. Hogan's study focuses on the ANP from 1919 to 1945 detailing its relationship with its members and Barrett's role in realizing its success.

(020D) Knox, George L. Slave and Freeman: The Autobiography of George L. Knox. Edited by William B. Gatewood, Lexington, KY: University Press of Kentucky, 1979.

George L. Knox was born into slavery. After the civil war he settled in Indiana and entered politics. In 1892 Knox purchased The Indianapolis Freeman. In this personal narrative Knox details his life as a young slave and discusses his eventual rise to success as a businessman, politician, and newspaper publisher.

(021D) Ottley, Roi. The Lonely Warrior: The Life and Times of Robert S. Abbott. Chicago: Henry Rignery Co., 1955.

On May 5, 1905, Robert S. Abbott began publishing The Chicago Defender. By 1915 Abbott had built the Defender's circulation to 200,000 and had become one of the most influential Black men in America. In this objective biography, Ottley chronicles the life of Robert S. Abbott from his childhood in Georgia to his last year in Chicago at the helm of "The World's Greatest Weekly" newspaper.

(022D) Schuyler, George S. Black and Conservative: The Autobiography of George S. Schuyler. New Rochelle, N.Y.: Arlington House, 1966.

For many years George S. Schuyler was a columnist for the Pittsburgh Courier. His conservative views raised the ire of many Black leaders. In this candid autobiography, Schuyler describes his early life in Syracuse, New York, his stint as a soldier during World War I in a segregated unit, and his intellectual odyssey which led him to develop extremely conservative positions on politics and race relations.

(023D) Thornbrough, Emma Lou. T. Thomas Fortune: Militant Journalist. Chicago: University of Chicago Press, 1972.

T. Thomas Fortune was one of the most eminent Black journalists during the last decades of the nineteenth century and the early years of the twentieth century. He wrote for white dailies in New York City as well as edited the New York Age for many years. Thornbrough's biography delineates his public career as a militant and fighter for Black American justice.

(024D) Wells-Barnett, Ida B. Crusade for Justice: The Autobiography of Ida B. Wells. Edited by Alfreda Duster. Chicago: University Press, 1970.

Born to slave parents in 1862, Ida B. Wells, as a pioneering Black female newspaper woman, became one of the foremost spokespersons against lynching in the last decade of the nineteenth century and the first decades of the twentieth century. Edited by her daughter, Alfreda Duster, this work, published 39 years after her death, is a first-hand account of Ida B. Wells' experiences as a journalist and civil rights activist.

Significant Journal Articles

(025D) Chaudhary, Anju G. "Press Portrayals of Black Officials." Journalism Quarterly 57 (Winter 1980):636-641.

The campaign coverage given to Black officials from 1970 through 1977 in 19 white metropolitan daily newspapers is analyzed in this study. Limited to cities with Black populations over 200,000, coverage given to Black officials in the following newspapers is examined: The Washington Post; Baltimore News American; New Orleans Times-Picayune; Memphis Commercial Appeal; Dallas News; Houston Post; Birmingham News; San Francisco Chronicle; Los Angeles Times; St. Louis Globe-Democrat; Newark Star-Ledger; New York Post; Cleveland

Plain-Dealer; Philadelphia Inquirer; and Miami Herald.

(026D) Garland, Phyl. "The Black Press: Down But Not Out." Columbia Journalism Review (September/October, 1982):43-50.

Veteran journalist and Associate Professor at Columbia University's Graduate School of Journalism, Phyl Garland discusses reasons for the decline of The Pittsburgh Courier and other Black newspapers. Garland does, however, view the establishment of the new National Leader and the success of the Sacramento Observer as evidence of a revitalization and an upswing in the Black press.

(027D) Lyford, Joseph P. "Something New for Oakland." Columbia Journalism Review (January-February, 1981):44-49.

Black journalist Robert Maynard was hired as Editor-in-Chief by the Garnett Company to revitalize the deteriorating Oakland Tribune. Lyford profiles Maynard. He discusses his philosophy and management decisions which have been successful in developing The Oakland Tribune and its sister newspaper Eastbay-Today into two of the most dynamic and fastest growing newspapers on the West Coast.

(028D) Munson, Naomi. "The Case of Janet Cooke." Commentary 22 (August 1981):46-50.

When Washington Post Black reporter Janet Cooke admitted that her feature story about an eight year-old boy who was a heroin addict, entitled "Inside Jimmy's World," was a hoax, the Pulitzer Prize which had been awarded to her for the story was withdrawn. Naomi Munson reviews the facts in the case and comments on its implications for affirmative action, journalists and integrity in journalism.

(029D) Poindexter, Paula M.; Stroman, Carolyn. "The Black Press and the Bakke Case." Journalism Quarterly 58 (Summer 1980):262-268.

This study reports on a content analysis of the coverage of the Bakke Case by four Black newspapers: The Chicago Defender; The Los Angeles Sentinel; New York Amsterdam News; and The Atlanta Daily World. The first phase of the analysis was done on the four newspapers during the ten months prior to the U.S. Supreme Court's ruling on the Bakke Case. The second phase of the analysis of the four newspapers was conducted in the months following the U.S. Supreme Court's decision on the case. The content analysis of the four Black newspapers revealed that: (1) coverage was event-oriented; (2) display was minimal; (3) implications in the case were seldom discussed.

(030D) Trayes, Edward J. "Black Journalists on U.S. Metropolitan Daily Newspapers: A Follow-up Study." Journalism Quarterly 57(Winter 1979):711-14.

In 1968, 32 of 48 daily and Sunday metropolitan newspapers

in 16 of the largest U.S. cities reported on the number of Black journalists on their staffs. Only 108 (2.6%) out of 4,095 positions were held by Blacks. In 1978 Clay Harris and the American Society of Newspaper Editors surveyed many of the same newspapers to determine the number of Blacks in news executive, desk and photography positions. Analyzing the data from the two studies, Trayes concludes that the employment of Blacks on major white daily and Sunday newspapers has increased during the ten-year period. However, he observes that Blacks are still not represented on these newspapers in proportions to the Black populations in the cities where these newspapers are published. Neither are Black journalists employed in news executive positions in significant numbers.

(031D) Washburn, Pat. "New York Newspapers and Robinson's First Season." Journalism Quarterly 58(Winter 1981):636-644.

In 1947 Jackie Robinson made his debut as the first Black American to play in the major leagues. Most baseball club owners and sports writers did not want Robinson or any other Black American playing in the major leagues. This study is devoted to an examination of the sports pages of The New York Times, the New York Herald Tribune, and the New York Daily News for 44 days during the 1947 baseball season to determine the press' treatment of Jackie Robinson in his maiden season in the major leagues.

Selected Dissertations

(032D) Brown, Karen F. "The Black Press of Tennessee, 1865-1980." Ph.D. dissertation, University of Tennessee, 1982.

Since 1865, 112 Black newspapers have seen published in Tennessee. From 1865 to 1899, at least 35 Black newspapers were published in the state. Between 1900 and 1950 there were 52 Black newspapers published in Tennessee; from 1951 to 1980 the number dropped to 25. In 1980 only three Black newspapers were published in Tennessee. This study analyzes the growth and development of Black newspapers in Tennessee from 1865 when the Colored Tennessean began publication through 1980. It highlights and discusses the personalities and forces which influenced the Black press in Tennessee as well as its impact on the political, social, and economic life of Black Tennesseans.

(033D) Spofford, Timothy J. "Lynch Street: The Story of Mississippi's Kent State -- The May 1970 Slayings at Jackson State College." Ph.D. dissertation, State University of New York at Albany, 1984.

On May 15, 1970, student unrest erupted on the campus of Jackson State College in Jackson, Mississippi, eleven days after the campus killings at Kent State University in Ohio. Members of the Mississippi Highway Patrol and the Jackson City Police opened fire on a crowd of students in front of the women's dormitory. Two students were killed and thirteen wounded. This study is a "documentary narrative" of the unrest before and after the killings.

MAGAZINE JOURNALISM

Indexes and Guides

(034D) Daniel, Walter C. Black Journals of the United States. Westport, Conn.: Greenwood Press, 1982.

Over 100 Afro-American periodicals, published between 1827 and the 1980s, are profiled in this comprehensive and well-documented work. Arranged alphabetically by title, each entry contains the following items: (1) a substantive historical essay discussing the periodical's development, editorial policy, and persons who played key roles in its history; (2) a list of information sources about the periodical which include works that describe it, index sources, and location sources; and (3) facts relative to the periodical's publication history. Appendix A is a chronology of events in Black history related to the founding of Black journals. Appendix B is a geographic distribution of Black journals.

(035D) Grant, Mildred Bricker, comp., Indexes to the Competitor. Westport, Conn.: Greenwood Press, 1978.

Robert L. Vann, publisher of The Pittsburgh Courier, began publishing in January 1920, The Competitor, a general literary magazine oriented towards Black Americans. In The Competitor were published editorials, articles, poems, fiction and cartoons by many of the leading Afro-Americans intellectuals, scholars and writers of the day which addressed a broad array of problems and concerns of the Afro-American during the early 1920s. After eighteen months of publication and reaching a circulation of 65,000, The Competitor ceased publication because of economic difficulties. Mildred Bricker Grant's indexes to The Competitor opens the contents of this important periodical to scholars and researchers. The title index is arranged alphabetically by the titles of articles, cartoons, fiction, plays, and poetry with references to volume number, issue number and page. Arranged alphabetically letter-by-letter, the author - subject index lists references from author and subject to volume number, issue number, and pages.

(036D) Guide to Scholarly Journals in Black Studies. With an introduction by Gerald A. McWorter, University of Illinois. Chicago: Peoples College Press, 1981.

In this premier guide to Black scholarly journals information for librarians and perspective authors about 26 major journals is presented. Each citation includes the following items about each journal: (1) editor; (2) administrative or editorial board; (3) type of material published; (4) subject area; (5) where abstracted or indexed; (6) publisher; (7)

submission information; (8) style specifications; (9) guide to submitting articles; (10) disposition of manuscripts; (11) business address; (12) circulation; (13) frequency of publication; and (14) subscription rates. Dr. McWorter's introduction is an enlightening commentary on the status of article publishing by Black intellectuals in scholarly Black and white journals.

Treatises

(037D) Bullock, Penelope L. The Afro-American Periodical Press, 1838-1909. Baton Rouge: Louisiana State University Press, 1981.

In 1838 Black Americans made their debut to American Magazine journalism with the publication of two journals. The Mirror of Liberty, edited by David Ruggles, published its first number in New York City in July of that year. The National Reformer, the official organ of the American Reform Society, edited by William Whipper, who founded the Society, began publication in Philadelphia in September of 1838. Professor Bullock in this pioneering study traces the growth of Black-owned periodical publishing between 1838 and 1909, highlighting the forces which influenced its development. The work's valuable appendices include: (a) "Publication Data and Selected Finding - List for the Periodicals"; (b) "Chronology of the Periodicals"; and (c) "Geography of the Periodicals." An extensive bibliography on the Afro-American press and a splendid index enhance the reference value of this important study.

(038D) Johnson, Abby Arthur; Johnson, Robert Mayberry. Propaganda and Aesthetics: The Literary Politics of Afro-American Magazines in the Twentieth Century. Amherst, Mass: The University of Massachusetts Press, 1979.

The Afro-American magazine has been, unlike the Afro-American newspaper, a vehicle through which Afro-Americans could substantively correlate their response to the larger society. Focusing on Afro-American literary, political and cultural magazines published in the twentieth century, this unique study discusses the content and function of these publications, the editors and personalities which shape them, and specific issues in Afro-Americana which they addressed. Sixty-four magazines, a few of them owned by white Americans even though they were Black-oriented, are included in this study which spans the years from 1900 through the late 1970s.

(039D) Kornweibel, Theodore, Jr. No Crystal Stair: Black Life and the Messenger, 1917-1938. Westport: Conn.: Greenwood Press, 1975.

From 1917 to 1928, Chandler Owen and A. Phillip Randolph edited and published the Messenger, a monthly periodical. Denounced as a radical publication by Black and white moderates and conservatives, the Messenger, whose editors advocated economic improvement for Black Americans, covered a wide range of subjects such as: Black political participation; Black trade unionism; the Harlem Renaissance; anti-lynching; and the Garvey Movement. This study focuses on the rise, influence and decline of the Messenger. Kornweibel views the magazine as "a convenient starting point from which to examine the prospects for change" by Afro-Americans during and after World War I. Although the author paints vivid portraits of Owen and Randolph, too little light is shed on their intellectual development.

Significant Journal Articles

(040D) Atwater, Tony. "Editorial Policy of Ebony Before and After the Civil Rights Act of 1964." Journalism Quarterly 59(Spring 1982):87-91.

This study is a qualitative analysis of the editorial content of Ebony magazine on civil rights. Forty-eight editions of Ebony magazine, which were published between July, 1962 through June 1964 were analyzed to determine the magazine's treatment of civil rights before and after passage of the Civil Rights Act of 1964.

(041D) Joyce, Donald Franklin. "Magazines of Afro-American Thought on the Mass Market. Can They Survive?" American Libraries 7(December 1976):678-683.

Joyce opens the article by discussing the publishing histories of four Afro-American periodicals devoted to Black thought: The Colored American, 1900-1909; The Half-Century, 1916-1925; The Competitor, 1920-1921; and Abbott's Monthly, 1930-1933. In the remainder of the article he analyzes the forces surrounding the sucess of the first run of the Negro Digest, 1942-1951 and the popularity and ill-fate the second run of the Negro Digest/Black World which was revived in 1961 but folded in 1976.

(042D) Sentman, Mary A. "Black and White: Disparity in Coverage by Life Magazine from 1937 to 1972." Journalism Quarterly 60 (Autumn 1983):501-508.

A content analysis of 52 issues of Life Magazine was conducted for the years 1937, 1942, 1947, 1952, 1957, 1962, 1967 and 1972 to determine the amount of coverage Blacks received in this mass media publication. The number of pages devoted to Blacks was tabulated. Based on the data gathered, the following conclusions were made: (1) coverage of everyday Black life was markedly absent, while coverage of the everyday lives of white Americans was consistent and represented 2% of the total magazine's content; (2) coverage of Black America amounted to a very minute portion of the magazine's content, and (3) Life did not give its mass audience exposure to everyday Black life.

(043D) Soley, Lawrence. "The Effect of Black Models on Magazine Ad Readership." Journalism Quarterly 60(Winter 1983):686-690.

Using data from Starch INRA syndicated reports of ad readership,

Soley analyzes the effect on readers of Black models used in 27 issues of Time, Newsweek, Sports Illustrated, and U.S. News and World Report between 1975 and 1980. He concludes that ads with Black models, white models and no models have comparable readership scores.

Significant Dissertations

(044D) Kern, Marilyn Louise. "A Comparative Analyses of the Portrayal of Blacks and Whites in White-Oriented Mass Circulation Magazine Advertisements During 1959, 1969 and 1979." Ph.D. dissertation, University of Wisconsin - Madison, 1982.

By conducting a content analysis of advertisements in randomly selected issues of six white-oriented magazines published during 1959, 1969 and 1970, Dr. Kern examines the status of Blacks in advertisements before, during and after the Civil Rights Movement. Of the 1,431 advertisements analyzed in Time, Women's Day, Newsweek, Vogue, Sports Illustrated, and Esquire, only 49 contained identifiable Blacks. It was concluded that the greatest proportion of integrated advertisements appeared in these publications in 1969 during the Civil Rights Movement.

RADIO AND TELEVISION JOURNALISM

Reports, Studies and Treatises

(045D) Black Participation in Public Television: Awareness and Audience Development. Performed by Delta Sigma Theta, Inc. Jeanne Nøble, Project Director. Funded by a grant from the Corporation of Public Broadcasting. Washington: Corporation of Public Broadcasting, [1978?]

During late 1977 and early 1978, Delta Sigma Theta Sorority conducted a public television awareness and viewing audience development demonstration project involving Black Americans in eight cities: Miami; Chicago; Washington, D.C.; Philadelphia; Bay Area (San Francisco-Oakland); Dallas; Detroit; and New Orleans. The purpose of the project was to test selected strategies which were designed to increase Black awareness and participation in public television. This report summarizes the findings and conclusions of this project.

(046D) How Blacks Use Television for Entertainment and Information. A Survey Research Project conducted by the Booker T. Washington Foundation and Cablecommunications Resource Center-West. Springfield, Virginia: National Technical Information Service, 1978.

This report is the result of a multiphase research project conducted in 1975 to determine the impact of television viewing on Black Americans. Based on approximately 200 interviews, this study focuses on the "uses and gratifications dimensions of television viewing by Black Americans."

(047D) Jackson, Anthony W., ed. Black Families and the Medium of Television. Ann Arbor: Bush Program in Child Development and Social Policy, University of Michigan, 1982.

Jackson has compiled and edited papers presented at a conference entitled "Black Families and the Medium of Television" which was held at the University of Michigan. The eleven papers by scholars and practicioners of television discuss the portrayal of Black families on television and the portrayals' impact on society. Among the contributors are Tony Brown of "Tony Brown's Journal" and Stanley Robertson, another television professional.

(048D) MacDonald, J. Fred. Blacks and White TV: Afro-Americans in Television Since 1948. Chicago: Nelson-Hall Publishers, 1983.

In the early years of television, critics predicted that it had great potential for improving many of America's social ills, among them racial prejudice against Black Americans which had been fostered to some extent by other mass media. Has television improved the image of Black Americans in the American society? J. Fred MacDonald seeks to answer this question. He analyzes how the television industry has treated Black Americans in three periods of its development: 1948-1957; 1957-1970; and 1970-1981.

Significant Journal Articles

(049D) Koiner, Richard B. "The Black Image of TV." Television Quarterly 17(Summer 1980):39-46.

The highlights of Black participation in the television industry as performers, technicians and managers since the 1950s is surveyed by Koiner. He discusses the failures of early Black programs such as Nat "King" Cole's show in 1956, but points to the later successes of Bill Cosby in "I Spy," Robert Guillaume in "Benson," and Max Robinson as a national ABC anchorman, as evidence of the increase of Blacks in television as performers. The expanding opportunities for Blacks in managerial and technical positions in the industry are considered as well as Black ownership of TV stations.

(050D) Poindexter, Paula M.; Stroman, Carolyn A. "Blacks and Television: A Review of the Research Literature." Journal of Broadcasting. 25(Spring 1981):103-132.

Poindexter and Stroman analyze the empirical literature which appeared on Blacks and television between 1948 and 1978. In this review of the literature they test several propositions under the following four main headings: (1) Portrayals; (2) Television As A Source of Information; (3) Viewing Behavior; and (4) Effects. They conclude that the studies which have been done on Blacks and television are fragmentary. "It is clear from the hodgepodge of findings on blacks that we are in need of a research agenda which will aid in theory construction. We, therefore, propose a research agenda to guide us in understanding the relationship of Blacks and television."

(051D) Sanders, Charles L. "Has TV Written Off Blacks?" Ebony. 36(September 1981):114-118.

In discussing the number of Black-oriented TV shows which were canceled in 1981, Sanders points out that white investors didn't want to back them because they did not believe that they would make money, despite the fact that many "Black" TV series have made returns to the investors. In the 1981-82 television season, Sanders observes, only 30 Black actors would work on TV series. He laments the plight of many Black TV performers who would be forced into the unemployment lines because of this tragic situation.

(052D) Singleton, Loy A. "FCC Minority Ownership Policy and Non-Entertainment. Programming in Black-oriented Radio Stations." Journal of Broadcasting. 25(Spring 1981):195-201.

In 1978 the Federal Communications Commission adopted a policy which supported increased ownership of radio stations by minorities. This policy was based on the assumption that minority-owned radio stations would develop programming tailored to the needs and interests of minorities. To test the validity of this assumption, non-entertainment programming on Black-owned and non-Black-owned radio stations was compared in this study. The findings revealed that Black-owned radio stations did not necessarily provide more non-entertainment programming for Blacks than non-Black-owned radio stations.

(053D) Tan, Alexis S.; Tan, Gerdean. "Television Use and Self-Esteem of Blacks." Journal of Communications 29(Winter 1979): 129-135.

In 1970 Blacks were casted in 46% of all television programs and 10% of all television commercials. They generally portrayed characters of relatively high social status than in previous years. However, by 1973 the situation had changed. Blacks appearing in television roles had greatly diminished and, for the most part, the roles in which Blacks were cast were representative of lower socio-economic characters. Alexis and Gerdean Tan explore the effect of television viewing on the self-esteem of Blacks and whites. After interviewing 176 adult Blacks and 157 adult whites in Lubbock, Texas, they draw many conclusions. Two of them are: (1) "constant exposure to white-oriented TV entertainment programs or those which depict blacks in low status roles causes low-self esteem in black audiences"; and (2) "the evidence here shows that high TV entertainment viewing is accompanied by low self-esteem among black audiences in our sample, but not among whites."

(054D) Taylor, Henry; Dozier, Carol. "Television Violence, African-

Americans and Social Change." Journal of Black Studies. 14(December 1983):107-136.

Taylor and Dozier advance the thesis that television violence is used to control the potential militancy among Black Americans. They assert that this is achieved by projecting violent Black law enforcement officers on television programs as role models for Black youth. By glamorizing and over-representing Black law enforcement officers as an occupational type on television program, an attempt is being made to encourage Black Americans to view police work as a good career choice.

Selected Dissertations

(055D) McDermatt, Steven T. "The Influence of Communication on Black Children's Self-Concept." Ph.D. dissertation, Michigan State University, 1982.

In this study Dr. McDermatt surveyed 82 fourth and fifth grade Black students who viewed Black family shows on television. The study's objectives are to show the influence of these shows on the Black child's: (1) self esteem; (2) racial esteem; and (3) comparative esteem.

(056D) Jackson, Harold. "From 'Amos 'N' Andy to 'I Spy'; Chronology of Blacks in Prime Time Network Television Programming 1950-1964." Ph.D. dissertation, Michigan State University, 1982.

Jackson identifies and discusses the roles played by Black actors and actresses on prime time television from 1950 to the fall of 1964 between the hours of 7:00 p.m. and 11:00 p.m. This study reveals that 310 Black actors and actresses appeared on 8,500 hours of prime time television out of 62,000 hours of prime time television during the period of the study.

(057D) Jeter, James Phillip. "A Comparative Analysis of the Programming Practices of Black-owned, Black-Oriented Radio Stations and White-Owned, Black-Oriented Radio Stations." Ph.D. dissertation, University of Wisconsin-Madison, 1981.

The Federal Communications Commission (FCC) and other government agencies have put into practice various policies aimed at increasing the level of minority ownership of television and radio stations. Dr. Jeter examines these policies in the light of Black-oriented radio stations by analyzing their: (1) areas of news; (2) public affairs and other programming; (3) public service announcements; (4) commercial programming; and (5) playlists. Non-playlist areas were analyzed by quantitative data used by the FCC to ascertain the performance of licenscees.

(058D) Spalding, Norman W. "History of Black Oriented Radio in Chicago, 1929-1963." Ph.D. dissertation, University of

Illinois at Urbana-Champaign, 1981.

This historical and cultural analysis of Black-owned radio programming in Chicago between 1929 and 1963 documents how it was a major influence in changing the Black community during the period. Data for this study was obtained from personal interviews with disc jockeys, musicians, entertainers, radio station owners, producers, and promotion personnel in the recording and broadcast industries.

E.
Thomas Blue's Dream: Blacks in Libraries and Librarianship

DIRECTORIES

(001E) Black Caucus of the American Library Association. 1983-1985 Membership Directory of the Black Caucus of the American Library Association. 4th edition. Pomona, N. J.: (Dr. George C. Grant, Stockton State College, P. O. Box 403), Black Caucus of the American Library Association, 1984.

Listing the current members of the Black Caucus of the American Library Association, this directory cites the following items about each member: name; position title; work address; home address; and phone number. In addition to an alphabetical listing by surname, there are classified listings by state and type of library where the members are employed.

STUDIES ON BLACK LIBRARIANSHIP AND LIBRARY SERVICE TO BLACK AMERICANS

(002E) Library Conference, Atlanta University, 1941. Library Conference Held under the Auspices of the Carnegie Corporation of New York and the General Education Board, March 14-15, 1941. Atlanta: Atlanta University Library, 1941.

The establishment of the new school of Library Service, at Atlanta University, which eventually opened in September of 1941, was the occasion on this conference. Black and white library leaders presented papers on key areas of Black Librarianship and library service to Blacks. Among some of the papers presented were: "Questions for a New Library School," by A. M. Hostetter; "Education for Librarianship - A New Opportunity in the South," by Louis R. Wilson; and "Public Library Service and the Negro," by Eliza A. Gleason.

(003E) Black Librarian in the Southeast: Reminiscences, Activities Challenges. Papers presented for a colloquim sponsored by the School of Library Science, North Carolina Central University, October 8-9, 1976. Ed. by A. L. H. Phinazee. Durham, N. C.:

North Carolina Central University, 1980.

These papers, presented on the occasion of the 35th anniversary of the School of Library Service at North Carolina Central University, detail the history and activities of Black librarians, library educators and library school alumni and students who lived or were educated in the Southeast.

(004E) Clack, Doris H. Black Literature Resources: Analysis and Organization. New York: Dekker, 1975.

An analysis of the Library of Congress' List of Subject Headings to determine their relevance and relatedness to Black literature resources is the focus of this study. Clack observes that there is a lack of relatedness in some subject headings. She concludes by presenting three lists which will assist the librarian in the subject analysis of Black literature resources. They are: (1) "Classified List of Relevant Subjects Included in the Library of Congress Classification Schedules and Appropriate Subject Headings"; (2) "Relevant Library of Congress Subject Headings in Alphabetical Order"; and (3) "Non-Relevant Classification Notation and Subject Headings Used with Black Literature Resources."

(005E) Gleason, Eliza A. Southern Negro and the Public Library: A Study of the Government and Administration of Public Library Service to Negroes in the South. Chicago: University of Chicago Press, 1941. (University of Chicago Studies in Library Science).

In this landmark study Dr. Eliza Atkins Gleason, the first Black American awarded a doctorate in library science, surveyed the availability of public library service to Black Americans in the South from the late nineteenth century through 1940. Using the mail questionnaire, primary documents and secondary sources, Gleason documents the severely limited access which Black Americans had to public libraries in Southern cities, althought they paid taxes which contributed to the tax base that supported these public institutions.

(006E) Handbook of Black Librarianship. Comp. and ed. by E. J. Josey and Ann Allen Shockley. Littleton, Colorado: Libraries Unlimited, 1977.

Historical and contemporary facts about many areas of Black Librarianship are presented in this wide-ranging reference source. Among some of the topics covered are: (1) the contributions of pioneering Black librarians; (2) a chronology of events in Black librarianship from 1808 through 1977; (3) the histories of southern state library organizations for Black Americans; (4) historical accounts of current organizations for Black librarians; (5) statistical data on Black librarians; (6) library education in Black Colleges and Universities; and (7) significant collections of Black literature.

(007E) Josey, E. J., ed. The Black Librarian in America. Metuchen,

N. J.: Scarecrow Press, 1970.

Twenty-five prominent Black librarians, including the editor of this volume, pen essays describing the individual paths that they followed in becoming and being Black librarians in America. They spare no names in describing the racism they encountered in library school, professional organizations and libraries where they worked.

(008E) Josey, E. J., ed. What Black Librarians are Saying. Metuchen, N. J.: Scarecrow Press, 1972.

In this compilation of essays, Black librarians discuss a broad range of subjects relevant to Black librarianship and library service to Blacks. The work is divided in the following seven sections: (1) "A Theoretical But A Pragmatical Problem"; (2) "On Academic Libraries"; (3) "An Intellectual Freedom Question"; (4) "Critical Issues in Library Education"; (5) "Organizing for Professional Action"; (6) "Toward Better Public Library Service for Black People"; and (7) "Librarians as Perpetrators of Change".

(009E) Smith, Jessie Carney. Black Academic Libraries and Research Collections: A Historical Survey. Westport, Connecticut: Greenwood Press, 1977.

In developing this pioneering study of libraries in 85 historically Black colleges, this researcher utilized two methods of data gathering: the mail questionnaire sent to the library directors and presidents of the institutions; and in-depth personal interviews with these administrators. The resulting monograph is a detailed analysis of the history and contemporary status of these academic libraries - focusing on their general collections, Black collections, services, staffs and funding support.

(010E) Yocom, Frances. List of Subject Headings for Books By and About the Negro. New York: H. W. Wilson Co., 1940.

While working as a librarian at Fisk University in the 1930s, Frances Yocom prepared this list of subject headings to be used for books by and about Blacks. The first list of its kind to be developed, it was incorporated into the Library of Congress' List of Subject Headings shortly after its publication.

TREATISES AND COMMENTARIES ON BOOKS AND BOOK PUBLISHING BY AND ABOUT BLACK AMERICANS

(011E) Broderick, Dorothy M. Image of the Black in Children's Fiction. New York: Bowker, 1973.

Broderick analyzes 104 children's books containing Black characters published between 1827 and 1967 to determine how Blacks are portrayed. She concludes that Blacks were generally depicted as inferior human beings. They were presented in such stereotypes as "the happy slave," "the musical," "the superstitious," and the "primitive Black."

(012E) Joyce, Donald Franklin. Gatekeepers of Black Culture: Black-owned Book Publishing in the United States, 1817-1981. Westport, CT: Greenwood Press, 1983.

The first book-length study on Black-Owned book publishing, this work traces its growth and development from 1817 through 1981. It focuses on: organizations, religious denominations, colleges and universities and private firms which engaged in book publishing during the period covered. A detailed profile of each publisher is presented in the appendix.

(013E) MacCann, Donnarae; Woodard, Gloria, eds. Black Americans in Books for Children: Readings in Racism. Edited with an Introduction by Donnarae MacCann and Gloria Woodard, Metuchen, NJ: Scarecrow Press, 1972.

Twenty-five articles from eleven journals discussing racism in children's books are presented in this pioneering compilation. The contributors, who are librarians, publishers and educators, focus on racist's attitudes contained in nearly one hundred books selected by libraries and schools. Notable among the twenty-five selections are: Augusta Baker's "Guidelines for Black Books: An Open Letter to Juvenile Editors"; and Nancy Larrick's "The All-White World of Children's Books."

(014E) Rollins, Charlemae Hill. We Build Together: A Reader's Guide to Negro Life and Literature for Elementary and High School Use. 3rd rev. ed. Champaign, Ill.: National Council of Teachers of English, 1967.

The first edition of this book, which was published 1941, was the result of the pioneering efforts of Charlemae Hill Rollins, a Black Children's Librarian, to influence publishers and writers to portray Blacks in children's books objectively and with dignity. It was the first guide of recommended books for children about Blacks. This third edition, compiled by the NCTE Publications Committee under the direction of Charlemae Hill Rollins, is the expanded annotated list of books including titles published through 1966.

COLLECTIONS, PROCEEDINGS, COMMENTARIES AND TEXTBOOKS ON VARIOUS DIMENSIONS OF LIBRARIANSHIP

(015E) A Century of Service: Librarianship in the United States and Canada. Edited by Sidney L. Jackson, Eleanor B. Herling and E. J. Josey. Chicago: American Library Association, 1976.

Black American library leader E. J. Josey is one of the editors of this Centennial Year volume which is a collection of 18 essays discussing the growth and development of various areas of library service in the United States since 1876. Three of the essays are by prominent Black librarians. They are: "Service to Afro-Americans," by A. P. Marshall; "Service to the Urban Rank and File," by Hardy R. Franklin; "Services to Library Life Abroad," by Vivian D. Hewitt.

(016E) Churchwell, Charles D. Shaping of American Library Education. (A.C.R.L. Publication in Librarianship No. 36). Chicago: American Library Association, 1975.

Churchwell's history of library education covers the years between the two world wars, 1919 and 1939. He discusses the influence on library education of the American Library Association, Temporary Library Training Board, the ALA Board of Education for Librarianship, the Carnegie Corporation's Ten-Year Program, and the Association of American Library Schools.

(017E) Clack, Doris Hargrett, ed. The Making of a Code: The Issues Underlying AACR2. Papers given at the International Conference on AACR2, held March 11-14, 1979 in Tallahassee, Florida. Sponsored by the School of Library Science, Florida State University. Chicago: American Library Association, 1980.

Selected librarians from Canada, the United Kingdom and the United States were members of the Joint Steering Committee for the revision of the second edition of the Anglo-American Cataloguing Rules (AACR2) which was published in 1979. Implementation of AACR2 was delayed, however, until 1981. In an effort to give librarians an opportunity to establish a positive attitude toward the new code, the School of Library Science of Florida State University sponsored, under the direction of Black library educator, Doris Hargrett Clack, the International Conference on AACR2. The proceedings of the conference comprise this work. The fifteen papers presented are included under the following headings: (1) "Generalities"; (2) "Description"; (3) "Access Points"; and (4) "Looking Beyond the Rules."

(018E) Ethnic Collections in Libraries, Edited by E. J. Josey and Marva L. Deloach. New York: Neal-Schuman, 1983.

Containing 18 essays by librarians and specialists, this resource book focuses on identifying ethnic collections, discussing problems associated with their administration and suggesting strategies for their future development. Ethnic collection of four ethnic groups are considered: Native Americans; Asian Americans; Black Americans; and Hispanic Americans.

(019E) Frost, Carolyn O. Cataloging Materials: Problems in Theory and Practice, by Carolyn O. Frost. Edited by Arlene Taylor Dowell Littleton, Colo.: Libraries Unlimited, 1983.

In this textbook, Frost discusses the historical and theoretical development of nonbook cataloging. Aimed at library science students and practicing catalogers, it illustrates, using detailed examples, the application of the two major codes,

Anglo-American Cataloguing Rules, Second Edition (AACR2) and Jean Weihs' Nonbook Materials: The Organization of Integrated Collections, to the cataloging of non-book materials.

(020E) The Information Society: Issues and Answers. [Sponsored by] American Library Association's President's Commission for the 1977 Detroit Annual Conference. Ed. with a Preface and Introduction by E. J. Josey and a Foreword by Clara Stanton Jones. Phoenix, AZ: Oryx Press, 1978.

This collection of thirteen papers, focusing on the impact of technological, social and economic change on libraries, were originally presented at the President's Program of Clara Stanton Jones, the first Black President of the American Library Association, at the 1977 Annual Conference of the American Library Association which was held in Detroit.

(021E) International Handbook of Contemporary Development in Librarianship. Edited by Miles M. Jackson. Westport, Conn.: Greenwood Press, 1981.

This broad collection of essays and articles covers the history and contemporary developments in librarianship in many countries and regions throughout the world. Over 50 distinguished librarians and scholars discuss public, academic, special and school library developments in these countries and regions.

(022E) Josey, E. J., ed. New Dimensions for Academic Library Service. Metuchen, N.J.: Scarecrow Press, 1975.

In this collection of essays, twenty-five librarians discuss the initiatives taken by academic librarians in the wake of new trends in higher education which have produced new demands on academic libraries and diminished funding which has decreased academic library budgets. Of the twenty-five essays, the following nine were written by Black librarians: "The Library in Academia: An Associate Provost's View," by Charles D. Churchwell; "On the Cutting Edge of Change: The Community College Library/Learning Resource Center," by Louise Giles; "The Black College Library in a Changing Academic Environment," by Casper LeRoy Jordan; "Education for Academic Librarianship," by Ivan L. Kaldor and Miles M. Jackson; "The User-Oriented Approach to Reference," by Ann Knight Randall; "The Need for Multimedia in Serving Students," by Harry Robinson, Jr.; "The Cooperative College Library Center," by Hillis Dwight Davis; "Utilizing Public and Special Libraries to Serve Post-secondary Education," by Vivian D. Hewitt; and "The Academic Library in the Year 2000," by E. J. Josey.

(023E) Smith, Jessie Carney, ed. Ethnic Genealogy: A Research Guide. Westport, CT: Greenwood Press, 1983.

This well-edited collection of ten authoritative and substantive articles by librarians, historians and archivists covers various areas of ethnic genealogical research which will be useful to amateur and seasoned genealogists. The ten articles are:

"Librarians and Genealogical Research," by Russell E. Bidlack; "Basic Sources for Genealogical Research," by Jean Elder Cazort; "Library Records and Research," by Casper L. Jordan; "Researching Family History," by Bobby L. Lovett; "The National Archives and Records Service," by James D. Walker; "The Genealogical Society of Utah Library," by Roger Scanland; "American Indian Records and Research," by Jimmy B. Parker; "Asian-American Records and Research," by Greg Gubler; "Black American Records and Research," by Charles L. Blockson; "Hispanic-American Records and Research," by Lyman DePlatt.

SELECTED JOURNAL ARTICLES

(024E) Contemporary Black Librarians. American Libraries 9(February 1978):81-86.

Eleven prominent Black Librarians are profiled in this article. They are: Gwendolyn S. Cruzat, Professor, Library School, University of Michigan; James C. Partridge, Jr., Specialist, Maryland State Department of Education; Pamela Cash, Librarian, Johnson Publishing Co., William A. Miles, Assistant Deputy Director, Buffalo and Erie County Public Library; Harry Robinson, Jr., Director, Zale Library, Bishop College; Lucille C. Thomas, Assistant Director, Center for Libraries, Media and Telecommunications, New York City School Board; Dock Alexander Boyd, Associate Professor, Library School University of Alabama; Dianne McAfee Williams, Director, Bureau of Instructional Media Programs, Wisconsin Department of Public Instruction; Lelia G. Rhodes, Library Director, Jackson State University; Barbara H. Clark, Head, Mobile Services, Los Angeles Public Library; Gladis E. Pannell, Coordinator, School Library Media Services, Campbell County Schools, Rustburg, Virginia.

(025E) Deacon, Deborah A. "Art and Artifacts Collection of the Schomburg Center for Research in Black Culture: A Preliminary Catalogue." Bulletin of Research in the Humanities (Summer 1981):137-381.

This complete number of the Bulletin of Research in the Humanities is devoted to the Schomburg Center for Research in Black Culture. The "Front Matter" describes the opening ceremonies for the new building on September 27, 1980. Deborah Deacon, in her extensive article, describes the history behind the development of the Art and Artifacts Collection of the Schomburg Center. In her extensive catalogue of the collection, she presents a biographical sketch of the artist and a physical description of each item.

(026E) Jelks, Joyce E; Sikes, Janice W. "Approaches to Black Family History." Library Trends 32(Summer 1983):139-159.

Jelks and Sikes, special collections librarians at Atlanta Public Library, share their expertise in handling reference questions in Black genealogy. Their presentation is divided into six sections: (1) an assessment of the reference interview; (2) a discussion of standard reference works in Black History; (3) referrals for the researcher; (4) documentation beyond Black family history; and (6) a bibliography of useful sources in Black genealogy.

(027E) Josey, E. J. "Can Library Affirmative Action Succeed? The Black Caucus of ALA Surveys Minority Librarians in 22 Leading Libraries." Library Journal 100(January 1, 1975):28-31.

In 1974 the Black Caucus of the American Library Association conducted a survey of 12 public library systems and 12 university library systems to determine the status of Black librarians in these systems. The respondents to the questionnaire were Black and minority professional librarians who provided evidence that affirmative actions programs involving Black and minority librarians were far from being realized in most of the library systems surveyed.

(028E) Josey, E. J. "Forging Coalitions for the Public Good: Excerpts from the June 27, 1984 Inaugural Address of E. J. Josey, the 101st President of the American Library Association." Library Journal. 109(August 1984):1393.

In these excerpts from his inaugural address, President E. J. Josey outlines the philosophy and programs of his presidency. He urges librarians, in the face of conservative forces seeking to advance the concept that "information is not a free good," to establish coalitions with national and local organizations, businesses, labor unions and congressmen to make information and knowledge accessible to all Americans in the interest of the "public good."

(029E) Kalisa, B. G. "Multi-ethnic Children's Books in the U.S.A.-An Examination of Contemporary Books about the African-American Experience." [presented at IBBY Conference, 1982]: Bookbird 20(1982):18-22.

During the late 1960s and the early 1970s, most of the children's books published about Blacks were written by white authors. Many of these books stereotyped the Black experience. Fortunately, today the majority of children's books about Blacks are written by Black authors. The themes and illustrations of twelve unique children's books about Blacks, which present realistic portrayals and contain positive illustrations, are examined. They are: Ashanti to Zulu, by Margaret Musgrove, illus. by Leo and Diana Dillion (1977); The Friends, by Rosa Guy (1973); Talk About a Family, by Eloise Greenfield, illus. by James Calvin (1978); Childtimes, by Eloise Greenfield (1979); Grandmama's Joy, by Eloise Greenfield, illus. by Carole Byard (1980); The Twins Strike Back, Valerie Flurnoy, illus by Diane de Groat (1980); The Best Time of Day, by Valerie Flurnoy, illus. by George Ford (1978); Daddy Is a Monster Sometimes, by John Steptoe (1980); Ride the Red Cycle, by Harriet G. Robinet, illus. by David Brown (1980); Cornrows, by Camille Yarbrough, illus. by Carole Byard (1979); Hi, Mrs. Mallory by Ianthane

Thomas, illus. by Ann-Toulmin-Roth (1979); Window Wishing, by Jeannette Caines, illus. by Kevin Brooks (1980).

(030E) Porter, Dorothy B. "Bibliography and Research in Afro-American Scholarship (Bibliographical Essay)." Journal of Academic Librarianship 2(May 1976):77-81.

In this essay Dr. Porter discusses the collecting activities of early Black and white bibliophiles who collected materials about Blacks, contemporary major Black literature collections, bibliographies and bibliographic aids and current scholarship being conducted in Black literature bibliography.

(031E) Porter, Dorothy B. "The Organized Educational Activities of Negro Literary Societies, 1828-1846." Journal of Negro Education 5(October 1936):555-576.

Surveying the leisure time educational activities of free Blacks in the North before the Civil War, Porter, in this classic study describes the development of early subscription libraries by Black literary societies. These literary societies, she observes, generally supported their libraries by charging members a fee when they joined and assessing them regular dues.

(032E) Shaw, Spencer G. "Charlemae Hill Rollins, 1897-1979, in Tribute." Public Libraries 21(Fall 1982):102-4.

In this speech delivered at the Second Charlemae Hill Rollins Colloquium at North Carolina Central University, fellow children's librarian and library educator, Spencer G. Shaw, commemorates the contribution of Charlemae Hill Rollins to children's librarianship and to humanity.

(033E) Stevenson, G. "Race Records: Victims of Benign Neglect in Libraries" Wilson Library Bulletin. 50(November 1975):224-232.

It is estimated that around 15,000 titles of race records, featuring famous and Black vocalists, were recorded between 1900 and 1950. During the peak recording years, 1926 through 1930, about 500 titles were issued annually. Stevenson observes that too few librarians have attempted to collect and preserve these recordings, which represent a rich contribution to American culture. He urges the library profession to begin to take an active role in the preservation, restoration, organization and access of race records. To assist practicing librarians, Stevenson cites record companies which are reissuing some race records as well as literary sources which discuss their significance to the development of American music.

(034E) Wilkins, John. "Blue's 'Colored' Branch: A "Second Plan" that Became a First in Librarianship: ALA Centennial Vignette No. 12. American Libraries 7(May 1976):256-257.

The "Colored Branch" of Louisville Free Public Library was open in 1905 in rented rooms under the direction of Rev. Thomas F. Blue.

(035E) Yuell, Phyllis. "Little Black Sambo: The Continuing Controversy." School Library Journal 22(March 1976):71-5.

Recounting the facts surrounding the writing and eventual success of Helen Bannerman's The Story of Little Black Sambo, Yuell focuses on the history of the controversy and protest against the use of the book by children's librarians which was begun by Charlemae Hill Rollins in 1941 and continued through the 1970s.

SELECTED DISSERTATIONS

(036E) Conley, Binford H. "A Study of Performance as Measured by Selected Indicators and Its Relationship to User Satisfaction and Resource Allocation in Five 1890 Land Grant Institution Libraries." Ph.D. dissertation, Rutgers University, 1981.

In this study, the Public Library Measurement Study was adopted to the academic library environment and used to measure performance, resource allocation, and user satisfaction in five 1890 land-grant institution libraries. It was found that a self-administered performance appraisal study of this kind was only feasible for a small academic library.

(037E) Deloach, Marva L." The Higher Education Act of 1965, Title II-B: The Fellowships for Training in Library and Information Science Programs: Its Impact on Minority Recruitment in Library and Information Science Education." Ph.D. dissertation, University of Pittsburgh, 1980.

In this study, DeLoach surveyed seventy Title II B grantee institutions to access the impact of Title II B programs on increasing the number of minority librarians in the profession. Deans and Directors, it was learned, felt that Title II B did have a positive impact on minority recruitment. DeLoach observed, however, that one of the problems which weakened the program was the hasty selection process used to acquire fellowship recipients.

(038E) Grant, George C. "Attitudes of Higher Education Library Administrators Toward the Adequacy of Middle State Association Library Evaluation Criteria and Processes." Ph.D. dissertation. University of Pittsburg, 1982.

Library administrators at 206 senior colleges and universities were surveyed with a questionnaire in which they were asked to rate twenty library evaluation criteria, seven evaluation processes, and six suggested changes in those criteria which the Middle States Associate used in its accrediting process. It was revealed that among the academic library administrators there was not dissatisfaction with present criteria and processes used by the Association in its accrediting process.

(039E) Matthews, Geraldine O. "The Influence of Ranganathan on Faceted Classification." Ph.D. dissertation, Case Western Reserve University, 1980.

S. R. Ranganathan, the late famous Indian librarian, was a pioneer in the development of faceted classification. Analyzing S. R. Ranganathan's published and unpublished works, which include editions of the Colon Classification, faceted classification and unpublished letters from 1930 to 1970, Dr. Matthews attempts to investigate his influence on faceted classification.

(040E) Merriman, Maxine Modell. "Augusta Baker: Exponent of the Oral Art of Storytelling; Utilizing Video As a Medium." Ph.D. dissertation, Texas Woman's University, 1983.

The intent of this study is threefold: (1) to ascertain whether there is a correlation between a storyteller's style and personality and the types of stories selected; (2) to analyze the premise that a live audience has an impact on the quality of storytelling; and (3) to preserve Augusta Baker's storytelling style and philosophy by producing a video-tape of Ms. Baker telling two stories and being interviewed. Augusta Baker, a Black children's librarian, was the former Coordinator of Work With Children for New York Public Library and an outstanding storyteller.

(041E) Williams, Barbara J. "A Study of Academic Library Relationships and the Institutional Self-Study in Selected 1890 Land-Grant Colleges and Universities." Ph.D. dissertation, Rutgers University, 1980.

The 1890 land-grant institutions are historically and publicly supported Black colleges and universities in several southern states. In this study, Dr. Williams attempts to determine whether academic librarians, administrators and faculty at a select number of these institutions viewed the regional accrediting process, using the self-study, as establishing and/or strengthening academic library relationships.

F.
Shuckin', Jokin', and Jivin': Blacks in Folklore

BIBLIOGRAPHIES

(001F) Ferris, William R., Jr. Mississippi Black Folklore: A Research Bibliography and Discography. Jackson, Mississippi: University Press of Mississippi, 1971.

Mississippi is rich in Black folklore. This extensive, but unannotated bibliography and discography, focuses on several aspects of Black Mississippi folklore as well as general Black folklore. It contains citations to books, journal articles, recordings and films.

(002F) Szwed, John F.; Abrahams, Roger D. Afro-American Folk Culture: An Annotated Bibliography of Materials from North, Central and South America and the West Indies. Philadelphia: Institute for the Study of Human Issues, Inc., 1978.

This comprehensive two-volume bibliography covers materials about Afro-American folk culture in more than twelve countries in the Western Hemisphere. Including works written in more than six languages, it contains citations to works such as non-fiction monographs, journal articles, pamphlets, novels, poetry, phonograph record notes and drama. The cut-off date for all publications cited is December 31, 1977. The primary arrangement is by geographical areas in the Western Hemisphere. Countries are arranged alphabetically within each geographical area. Broad subject indexes to each volume provide for cross cultural and indepth access to citations on many subjects in Afro-American folk culture.

COMMENTARIES AND TREATISES ON BLACK FOLKLORE

(003F) Abrahams, Roger. "Deep Down in the Jungle." Negro Narrative Folklore from the Streets of Philadelphia. Rev. ed. Chicago: Aldine, 1970.

Centering on the function and tradition of oral performances by one group of Black men in a lower class community of Philadelphia, the study analyzes the content and style of key words, jokes and toasts in lower class Black urban life. The performances are analyzed in the light of changing attitudes and perspectives of lower class urban Blacks. In "Section 1: The Tellers," the neighborhood, the role of verbal creativity in the Black community, and the performers are described and analyzed. "Section 2: The Texts," is devoted to: (a) discussing style and performance of the performers; and (b) presenting the stories of the performers.

(004F) Abrahams, Roger D. The Man-of-Words in the West Indies. Baltimore: John Hopkins University Press, 1983.

According to Abrahams, there are two kinds of men-of-words in the West Indies. They are the "good talkers" and the "good arguers." The "good talkers" traditionally perform at festive occasions and the "good arguers" at solemn events. In this group of essays, Abraham discusses the role and performance technique of these men-of-words in West Indian culture.

(005F) Bell, Michael J. The World from Brown's Lounge: An Ethnology of Black Middle Class Play. Champaign: University of Illinois Press, 1983.

Describing the artistic and creative language used by Black middle class habitues of a Philadelphia bar to communicate and entertain each other, this unique study of Black oral folklore deals with the immediate present, instead of the past. The informants are "actors" who create folklore through their speech and actions while at leisure in Brown's Lounge in Philadelphia.

(006F) Dundes, Alan, ed. Mother Wit from the Laughing Barrel: Readings in the Interpretation of Afro-American Folklore. New York: Garland, 1981.

These selected essays and commentaries by folklorists, sociologists and other sepcialists discuss critical issues related to the study of Afro-American folklore. They are divided into the following eight sections: (1) "Folk and Lore," essays discussing the positive and negative attitudes toward Afro-American folklore; (2) "On Origins," research commentaries that consider the origin of Afro-American folklore; (3) "Folk Speech," selections discussing traditional names and slang; (4) "Verbal Art," essays analyzing the various forms of word-play such as "signifying" and "playing the dozens."; (5) "Folk Beliefs," (6) "Folk Music," commentaries examining Afro-American folk music; (7) "Folk Narrative," selections investigating various narrative forms including folktales, legends and memorates; and (8) "Folk Humor," essays devoted to analyzing traditional folklore.

(007F) Fry, Gladys-Marie. Night Riders in Black Folk History. Knoxville: University of Tennessee Press, 1975.

Southern whites, especially plantation owners, were fearful of slave insurrections. To deter Blacks from congregating secretly at night, many slave masters engineered the spreading of ghost stories among slaves with the intent of arousing their superstitions and fear of the supernatural. In this seminal study, Gladys-Marie Fry, utilizing Black slave narratives and the accounts of Black informants, explores and documents the authenticity of the "ghost stories" and the effect that they had on slaves.

(008F) Hurston, Zora Neale. Mules and Men. Philadelphia: Lippincott, 1935 (reprinted) New York: Negro Universities Press, 1960.

This work by one of the earliest trained Black folklorists is a classic. Hurston returns to her native Eatonville and Polk County, Florida in 1927 and 1928 to collect folktales from old friends which she had heard as a child. She records the tales and gestures of her informants faithfully and with the ear of a writer. The second section of the work is centered around New Orleans where Hurston, sometimes at personal risks, collected voodoo tales. In this section, she describes voodoo rituals, the power of root doctors and their prescriptions.

(009F) Jackson, Bruce, ed. The Negro and His Folklore in Nineteenth Century Periodicals. Austin: University of Texas Press, 1967.

Including articles on Black folklore which appeared in journals from 1830 to 1900, this work is an excellent source on the attitudes white Americans held toward Black American folklore in the nineteenth century. The writers, who discuss such topics as Black religion, superstition, music, and dialect, are abolitionists, slaveholders and prominent white writers.

(010F) Levine, Lawrence. Black Culture and Black Consciousness: Afro-American Folk Thought from Slavery to Freedom. New York: Oxford University Press, 1978.

Utilizing hundreds of folkloristic documents, including songs, folktales, proverbs, aphorisms, verbal games, and oral poems, this study analyzes the development of Afro-American folk thought in the United States from the antebellum period through the late 1940s. It presents evidence to illustrate that the African captives and generations of Afro-Americans who followed kept alive through their folk culture significant aspects of their African heritage.

(011F) Puckett, Newbell Niles. Folk Beliefs of the Southern Negro. Chapel Hill: University of North Carolina Press, 1926 (Reprinted, New York: Negro Universities Press, 1968).

Originally published in 1926, this classic study on Black

folk life, centering on folklore and superstition, presents and discusses twenty-five hundred folk beliefs of southern Blacks. An attempt is made to show the origins of these beliefs and to establish some general principles governing the transmission of folklore among southern Blacks. Over four hundred informants were used to collect data as well as questionnaires which were sent to Black colleges in the South.

(012F) Smith, Michael P. Spirit World. Pattern in the Expressive Folk Culture of Afro-American New Orleans. Photographs and Journal by Michael R. Smith. New Orleans: New Orleans Urban Folklore Society, 1984.

The contemporary folk culture of the Black community of New Orleans is presented in photographs and an explanatory commentary in this exhibit catalog. The photographs were taken between 1968 and 1983 and include scenes from religious cult ceremonies and services, funeral parades, Mardi Gras parades and exhibits. Smith's commentary explains the history of each ceremony and discusses its significance in the Black folk culture of New Orleans.

VOODOO/HOODOO

(013F) Bourguignon, Erika. Possession. San Francisco: Chandler and Sharpe, 1976.

Voodoo practices in Haiti are discussed and analyzed substantially in this work. Its focus, however, is on the notion of "possession." "Possession" is presented as a type of belief and as "possession trance" as a mode of behavior.

(014F) Deren, Maya. Divine Horsemen: Voodoo Gods of Haiti. Foreword [by] Joseph Campbell. New York: Dell Publishing Co., 1970.

Various aspects of voodooism in Haiti are discussed in this survey. Deren describes the role and function of voodoo gods, dances, and rituals as well as the hierarchy in Haitian voodoo. A glossary of Creole terms used in Haitian voodoo is included.

(015F) Haskins, Jim. Voodoo and Hoodoo: Their Traditions and Craft as Revealed by Actual Practitioners. New York: Stein and Day, 1981.

Haskins traces the history of Voodoo and Hoodoo from their roots in Africa to present day practices in the New World. He presents authentic recipes from voodoo and hoodoo practitioners related to: (1) doing evil; (2) doing good; (3) matters of law, and (4) matters of life. An excellent bibliography is included.

(016F) Mitchell, Faith. Hoodoo Medicine: Sea Islands Herbal

Remedies. Berkeley: Reed, Cannon and Johnson Co., 1978.

In the first section of this work, Mitchell presents a brief history of the Sea Islands from 1640 to 1974 focusing on the Black medical system. She discusses how transported African slaves adapted their herbal hoodoo medical knowledge to the new environment of the Sea Islands. The second section of this work is devoted to a detailed description of various medicinal plants used in the Sea Islands by Blacks.

(017F) Tallant, Robert. Voodoo in New Orleans. New York: Collier, 1974, 1946.

Voodoo practices in New Orleans from the early nineteenth century to the mid-twentieth century are described in this work. The life and escapades of the flamboyant Marie Laveau, the city's mulatto reigning voodoo queen from 1826 to 1881, are presented in detail as well as the adventures of lesser practitioners of voodooism in the city's colorful history.

(018F) Watson, Wilbur, ed. Black Folk Medicine: The Therapeutic Significance of Faith and Trust. With a Foreword by Doris Y. Wilkinson. With an Afterword by Nelson McGee. New Brunswick, N.J.: Transaction Books, 1984.

Home remedies have been a mainstay of the Black community. This anthology focuses on the systems, philosophies and character of the relationship between the patient and practitioner in Black folk medicine. It includes such commentaries as: "Folk Medicine and Older Blacks in Southern United States," by Wilbur H. Watson; "Poverty, Folk Remedies and Drug Misuse Among the Black Elderly," by Benny J. Primm; and "Doctor Can't Do Me No Good: Social Concomitants of Health Care Attitudes and Practices Among Elderly Blacks in Isolated Rural Populations," by J. Herman Blake.

COLLECTIONS ILLUSTRATIVE OF THE BLACK ORAL FOLKLORE TRADITION

(019F) Brewer, John Mason. American Negro Folklore. Illustrations by Richard Lowe. Chicago: Quadrangle Books, 1968.

This is a general collection of Afro-American folklore items. It includes: tales, sermons and prayers, songs, personal experiences, superstitions, proverbs, rhymes, riddles, names, and children's rhymes and pastimes.

(020F) Courlander, Harold. A Treasury of Afro-American Folklore. New York: Crown Publishers, Inc., 1976.

The folklore traditions in oral literature, music, religion, myths, legends, myth-legends, human tales, animal tales, near-epics and recollections of historical happenings of persons of African descent throughout the Western Hemisphere are included in this comprehensive anthology. Illustrated with thirty photographs, this work has appendices with several African stories which may be viewed as prototypes of Afro-American folk tales.

(021F) Dance, Daryl. Shuckin' and Jivin': Folklore from Contemporary Black Americans. Bloomington, Ind.: Indiana University Press, 1978.

Five hundred and sixty-five traditional prose narratives anecdotes, folk songs, folk verses, and accounts of individual experiences are presented in this general collection of Afro-American oral folklore. Most items were transcribed verbatim by the author who taped informants' personal performances. All informants were Afro-Americansliving in Virginia. Annotations are included for each item giving the place and date of the taping. Biographical sketches of the major informants and contributors are found in the appendix.

(022F) Dorson, Richard, ed. American Negro Folktales. Greenwich: Fawcett Publishers, 1967.

Many of the editor's previously published folktales are included in this collection. Among some of them are: Negro Tales from Pine Bluff, Arkansas and Calvin, Michigan, (Bloomington, Indiana: Indiana University Press, 1958) and several tales reprinted from folklore journals.

(023F) Hughes, Langston; Bontemps, Arna, eds. The Book of Negro Folklore. New York: Dodd, Mead, and Co., 1958.

A variety of Black folklore is presented in this anthology. It includes animal tales, animal rhymes, slave narratives, preacher tales, ghost stories, voodoo tales, sermons, prayers testimonials, spirituals, gospel songs, pastime rhymes, ballads, blues, work songs, street cries, playsongs and games, poetry in the folk manner, and prose in the folk manner.

(024F) Pruitt, Jakie; Cole, Everett. As We Lived: Stories by Black Storytellers. Burnet, Texas: Eakin Press, 1982.

Because slaves were forbidden to learn to read and write, the record of important episodes in their lives were passed from generation to generation orally. This collection of stories told in the oral tradition by five aged Blacks in the backwoods of South Central Texas describe life altering experiences in the lives of the storyteller's ancestors. These stories, illustrative of the oral tradition among many Blacks, are examples of the rich unrecorded history of Black America which fill a vacuum in American regional history.

(025F) Spalding, Henry D., ed. Encyclopedia of Black Folklore and Humor. Introduction by J. Mason Brewer. Illustrated by Rue Knapp. Middle Village, New York: Jonathan David Publishers, 1972.

Spalding successfully attempts to relate Afro-American folklore to orthodox history in this sprawling work. His selection of items emphasizes the humorous elements in Afro-American folklore. The 1,500 folktales, jokes, folksongs, poems, children's rhymes, proverbs, maxims, superstitions, soul-food recipes and excerpts from diaries and letters included are divided among eight books and 47 sub-classifications.

(026F) Thompson, Rose. Hush, Child! Can't You Hear the Music. Collected by Rose Thompson. Edited by Charles Beaumont. Foreword by John Stewart. Athens: University of Georgia Press, 1982.

Twenty-five unique folktales which were told by rural Georgia Blacks to Rose Thompson, a white farm extension agent, who worked in rural Georgia among Blacks, who loved and respected her. Each story, edited for clarity, is introduced by Ruth Thompson who describes the circumstances under which she collected it. The forward by John Stewart discusses Ms. Thompson's collecting technique and her insights into collecting folktales among Georgia Blacks.

(027F) Wepman, Dennis, et. al. The Life: The Lore and Folk Poetry of the Black Hustler by Dennis, Ronald B. Newman, Murray B. Benderman. Philadelphia: University of Pennsylvania Press, 1976.

Toasts are Black oral folk poems depicting hustlers in Black urban sporting life. Recited at parties, in pool halls and on street corners by individuals who excel in their performance, toasts are a dying genre in Black urban folklore. Like all folk poetry, toasts are instructive as well as entertaining. They are anonymous and seldom written. This collection of toasts was collected in four prisons in New York State between 1953 and 1967. The informants were inmates who were skilled in reciting toasts.

SIGNIFICANT JOURNAL ARTICLES

(028F) Dance, Daryl C. "Tuning in the Boiler and the Cotton Patch: New Directions in the Study of Afro-American Folklore." [review article] CLA Journal 20(June 1977):547-53.

In this paper, originally presented at the Thirty-Seventh Annual Convention of the Collge of Language Association in Jackson, Mississippi on April 21, 1977, Dance critically accesses the works which have been published on Afro-American folklore. She notes that the majority of this research has been done by white scholars and that much of this work reflects their own biased perceptions. Dance cites some excellent works which have appeared by Black scholars in the field and urges more Blacks to engage in research in Black folklore.

(029F) Flusche, M. "Joel Chandler Harris and the Folklore of Slavery." Journal of American Studies 9(December 1975): 347-63.

Slave folklore does provide valuable insight into the slave's view of slavery. Flusche observes that historians using special techniques should examine slave folklore. He critically assesses Joel Chandler Harris' method of collecting and reporting slave folktales and concludes that Harris' Black folktales did not present a complete picture of how slaves viewed themselves and the world around them.

(030F) Harner, Thurmon. "Playing the Dozens: Folklore as Strategies for Living." Quarterly Journal of Speech 69(February 1983):47-57.

"Playing the Dozens" is an aggressive verbal contest played by Black adolescents in which obscence language is used to vilify the relatives of the contestants. In this essay Garner analyzes this kind of obscence folkloric speech pattern in a community fictiously named "Tattler." Employing participant-observer techniques, he concludes that "Playing the Dozens" provide the participants with a vehicle or strategy for rhetorically resolving interpersonal conflicts.

(031F) Golden, Kenneth M. "Voodoo in Africa and the U.S." American Journal of Psychiatry, 134(1977):1425-27.

The practice of hexing is not a phenomenon confined to the rural South. Its existence is also in many Northern communities. Hexing is a voodoo practice which has its origins in Africa as a voodoo practice, this article focuses on its use and capabilities in the present day United States.

(032F) Hill, Mildred A. "Common Folklore Features in African-American Literature." Southern Folklore Quarterly 39(June 1975):111-133.

Hill investigates folklore features from African heritage which recur in Black literature. Her discussion centers on three areas of folklore: magic and superstition; story-telling; and folk-sayings.

(033F) Rich, Carolyn R. "Born With a Veil: Black Folklore in Louisiana." Journal of American Folklore 89(July 1976)): 328-31.

Presumbly good luck attends the child who is born with "the veil." The child born with the veil has the power to see and hear ghosts and be able to predict the future. This notion, according to Rich, persists among Blacks in the South. Rich observes:

> "...today in the Deep South the notion persists chiefly among Blacks."

(034F) Rickford, J. R.; Rickford, A. E. "Cut-Eye and Suck-Teeth: African Words and Gestures in New World Guise." Journal of American Folklore 89(July 1976):294-309.

"Cut-eye" and "Suck-teeth" are two compound words describing two gestures which are African in origin. They are commonly used by Blacks in the New World. Data on the meaning and usage of these two gestures were collected and analyzed by the author. Black and white informants were used for the study from several Caribbean countries and the United States.

(035F) Roberts, John W. "Stackalee and the Development of a Black Heroic Idea." Western Folklore 42(July 1983):179-190.

Stacklee, since the late nineteenth century, has been a prominent folk hero in Afro-American folklore. Unlike folk heroes in Anglo-American folklore who are perceived as "the noble robber," Stackalee is perceived by Black Americans as "the avenger." Stackalee is a folk hero because of the terror and cruelty surrounding him. He, as Roberts observes, is not used as a role model, but embodies the heroic idea for Black people. Roberts traces and discusses the development of Stackalee in Black folklore from the late nintienth century through the 1980s. Among the conclusions which Roberts draws is:

> "Stackalee symbolizes the black urban male's idea of heroism. In one sense, he provides escape from the reality of urban existence, but this avenue of escape is never portrayed as ideal or even desirable."

(036F) Willis, Miriam DeCosta. "Folklore and the Creative Artist: Lydia Cabrera and Zora Neale Hurston." CLA Journal 27(September 1983):81-90.

Lydia Cabera and Zora Neale Hurston were two contemporary women writers and folklorists who utilized the themes, stylistic devices and characters of the Black oral tradition in their creative works. Cabera, a Cuban, centered her writings on Afro-Cuban folklife, while Hurston's writings reflected Afro-American folklife. In this article, Willis discusses the similarities and differences in the folkloric writings of these two authors.

SELECTED DISSERTATIONS

(037F) David, John R. "Tragedy in Ragtime: Black Folktales from St. Louis." Ph.D. dissertation, St. Louis University, 1976.

David presents in this study a historical Stackalee in the person of Lee Shelton. Shelton was a St. Louis political figure who was prominent around the turn of the century. He shot Billy Lyons, another St. Louis politician, in a political dispute.

(038F) Bell, Michael E. "Pattern, Structure, and Logic in Afro-American Hoodoo Performance." Ph.D. dissertation, Indiana University, 1980.

Hoodoo practices are generally regarded by most scholars as being devoid of logic. Bell, after closely examining the works on Hoodoo by folklorist Harry Middleton Hyatt, determines that there is structure and logic in hoodoo practices. The hoodooist, he concludes, can perform creatively and yet work within a structure governed by traditional rules or logical propositions.

(039F) Stockard, Janice L. "The Role of the American Black Woman in Folktales: An Interdisciplinary Study of Identification and Interpretation." Ph.D. dissertation, Tulane University, 1980.

The Black woman has generally been ignored in the study of Afro-American folklore. Sixty-one Afro-American folktales which contain Black Women characters are analyzed in this study. The methodology employed uses several analytical techniques from the disciplines of anthropology, English, history, and sociology as well as the method of identification and interpretation, a new development in folklore analysis. The investigator's findings reveal that the Black woman is a major character in Afro-American folklore, and that she is composed of many more sociocultural components than had been formally observed.

G.
Jist Say'n' It: Blacks in Linguistics

BIBLIOGRAPHIC WORKS

(001G) Brasch, Ila W.; Brasch, Walter M. A Comprehensive Annotated Bibliography of Black American English. Baton Rouge: Louisiana State University Press, 1974.

Including about 2,000 entries to books, journal articles, pamphlets and reports on American Black English, this work is the most comprehensive bibliography on the subject. Over 80 per cent of the entries are annotated. The following types of entries on or related to Black American English are represented: (1) research studies; (2) general studies; (3) pedagogy; (4) general interest articles; (5) reviews of articles and books; (6) folklore; (7) slave narratives; (8) literature; (9) material related to Black American English; (10) literature on the disadvantaged related to Black American English. Entries are arranged alphabetically by author. There is, however no subject index.

CONFERENCE PROCEEDINGS AND SEMINAR DELIBERATIONS

(002G) Black English: A Seminar. Edited by Deborah Sears Harrison [and] Tom Trabasson. Hillsdale, New Jersey: L. Erlbaum Associates, 1976.

Fifteen essays by specialists and students in Black English, who participated in a seminar held at Princeton University in 1973 are presented in this collection. Black English is discussed from the following four perspectives: its historical origins, its usage, its definition; and its implications. Among some of the essays included are: "Toward the Parameters of Black English," by Gilbert A. Sprauve; "Pidgins, Creales, and the Origins of Vernacular

Black English," by Elizabeth Class Traugott; "Black English and Black Folklore," by Danille Taylor; and "Linguistic Relativity: Any Relevance to Black English?" by John B. Carroll.

(003G) Jackson, Alma F. The Uses of Negative Concord by Ten College-Educated Blacks. Greensboro, N.C.: Reproduced and Distributed by the Interdepartmental Program in Linguistics, University of North Carolina, Greensboro, 1978.

The "negative concord" is the use of a negative to more than one indefinite. It is commonly used in the Black English vernacular speech of Black innter-city youth. An example of a "negative concord," according to Alma F. Jackson, is the following sentence: "You won't have no chance to say nothing to nobody." In this paper presented at the Southeastern Conference on Linguistics, March 1977, Jackson discusses the results of a study to determine whether a group of select college-educated Blacks used the "negative concord" in their speech. The informants for the study were ten Black graduate students at the University of North Carolina-Chapel Hill.

(004G) National Invitational Symposium on the King Decision, 1980, Wayne State University. Black English and the Education of Black Children and Youth: Proceedings of the National Invitational Symposium on the King Decision. Edited with an introduction by Geneva Smitherman. Detroit: Center for Black Studies, Wayne State University, 1981.

On July 12, 1979, U. S. District Judge Charles W. Joiner issued a ruling which required the Ann Arbor School District (Mich.) to devise a program whereby Black students in the District's Martin Luther King Junior High School who spoke Black English could successfully be taught standard English. The ruling implied that teachers at King Junior High School and similar schools must understand and work effectively with the problems associated with teaching lower class Black children who speak Black English. The National Invitation Symposium on the King Decision was a workshop designed for educators and decision makers to acquaint them with: (1) Black English; (2) problems associated with teaching a child or youth who speaks Black English; and (3) successful methods of teaching children and youth who spoke Black English. Keynoted with a speech by James Baldwin, the workshop included papers by noted educators and linguistics as well as task force reports and a list of recommendations.

DICTIONARIES

(005G) Dalgish, Gerard M. A Dictionary of Africanism: Contributions of Sub-Saharan, Africa to the English Language. Westport, CT: Greenwood Press, 1982.

This work is a dictionary of terms from the four African

language groups which have entered the general English-speaking vocabulary. Approximately 3,000 terms were collected which appeared frequently in a wide range of sources. These sources were African, Afro-American, American, British and Canadian publications.

(006G) Major, Clarence. Dictionary of Afro-American Slang. New York: International Publishing Co., 1970.

This glossary of over 2,500 entries defines many expressions which originated and are commonly used in the Black community. An explanation for each term is given in a one-line commentary which discusses its origin and meaning.

TREATISES AND COMMENTARIES

(007G) Baugh, John. Black Street Speech: Its History, Structure and Survival. Austin: University of Texas Press, 1983.

Black street speech is analyzed in this study. Baugh traces its history as reported in a variety of primary and secondary sources. Utilizing interviews conducted on informants, sometimes repeatedly, in Los Angeles, Philadelphia, Chicago and Texas, Baugh examines Black street speech focusing on its specialized lexical markings and alternation, unique grammatical usage, and phonological variation.

(008G) Black American English: Its Background and Its Usage in the Schools and Literature. Edited and Introduced by Paul Stoller. New York: Dell Publishing Co., 1975.

This anthology of eight essays by linguists, education specialists and folklorists, supplemented by selections from the published works of three Black writers, discusses and illustrates the linguistic, socio-political and literary concerns associated with Black speech. The discussion focuses on three areas of Black speech: (1) "History and Structure of Black Speech," (2) "Black Speech and Education"; and (3) "Black Speech and Literature".

(009G) Brasch, Walter M. Black English and the Mass Media. Amherst: University of Mass. Press, 1981.

This historical study, which centers on Black English in the mass media, is based on two hypotheses. They are: (1) "the only available evidence, historically, on the presence of Black English appears in the mass media in the various genres of fiction and non-fiction"; (2) "that mass media reflected the awareness, concern and knowledge of Black English through the years." This study examines and analyzes Black English documentation in the mass media in five periods from 1765 through 1981.

(010G) Dillard, J. L. Black English: Its History and Usage in the

United States. New York: Random House, 1972.

Although it treats the history of Black English substantively, this highly readable study considers the following aspects of Black English: (1) its structure; (2) how it differs from other varieties of American English; and (3) Black English and education. Included are a glossary of linguistic terms related to the study of Black English and an appendix on the pronunciation of Black English words.

(011G) Dillard, J. L. Lexicon of Black English. New York: Seabury Press, 1977.

This work is not a lexicon. It is a study of Black English vocabulary in selected domains. Each chapter is devoted to one domain. Among the domains covered are: sex and love-making; the Blues; and root work and conjure.

(012G) Dillard. J. L., ed. Perspectives on Black English. Hawthorne, N. J.: Mouton, 1975.

Leading linguists discuss many facets of Black English in twenty-one essays. The essays are grouped under four topics: (1) "Black English Dialectalogy: Theory and Method"; (2) "Black English and the Acculturation Process"; and (3) "Black English and Psycholinguistics." J. L. Dillard's "General Introduction: Perspectives on Black English" is a detailed, comprehensive bibliographic essay on studies and publications on Black English which appeared between the late 18th century and the mid 1970s.

(013G) Fasold, Ralph. Tense Marking in Black English: A Linguistic and Social Analysis with a chapter by Carolyn Kessler. Arlington, VA: Center for Applied Linguistics, 1972.

Fasold asserts that: "There is much to be learned about the theory of grammar if variation is taken into account. This study illustrates the principles of such variation theorists as William Labov and Charles-James Bailey. It is a detailed study of tense marking in Black English aimed at providing information on which pedagogical materials can be developed. Kessler's chapter on noun plural forms utilizes implication analysis which was proposed by David Camp. It has become an innovation in variation theory.

(014G) Fickett, Joan C. 'Merican, An Inner-City Dialect: Aspects of Morphemics, Syntax and Semology. Taos, N.M.: Printed by Deckerhoff's Print, 1975. (Studies in Linguistics, Occasional Papers, No. 13).

This study, using informants who were Black students at East High School in Buffalo, New York, reports on the dialect spoken by Black inner-city students. It discusses the morphemic, syntax and semology of the dialect which Fickett has named "'Merican."

(015G) Folb, Edith A. Runnin' Down Some Lines: The Language and Culture of Black Teenagers. Cambridge: Harvard University Press, 1980.

This ethnographic study focuses on the speech patterns and related lifestyles of Black teenagers in South Central Los Angeles. The vocabulary and idiomatic usages of these informants are subjected to sociolinguistic analysis which reveal insights into their world of experiences, their beliefs, attitudes and values. An extensive glossary of Black vernacular terms used by the teenage informants enhances this study.

(016G) Haskins, James; Butts, Hugh. The Psychology of Black Language. New York: Barnes and Noble, 1973.

From the vantage point of an educator and a psychologist, the development of language among Black Americans is considered in this rather unique work. It discusses: (1) the psychology of oppression among Black Americans and its relationship to the verbal behavior of Blacks; (2) the development of verbal behavior in Black children; and (3) the evaluation of various dialects among Blacks.

(017G) Holton, Sylvia W. Down Home and Uptown. Cranbury, N.J.: Fairleigh Dickinson University Press, 1984.

Black English as a literary language has been used in American fiction since the antebellum period. This study examines the presence of Black English in American fiction by: (1) discussing the dominant theories about the origins, development and present linguistic phenomenon of Black English; (2) reviewing the major linguistic studies on Black English which were done in the 1960s and 1970s; (3) presenting a literary discussion illustrating the ways the speech of Blacks has been presented in American fiction; (4) analyzing the dialect fiction portraying Blacks in the pre- and post-civil war periods;(5) considering the years of change in presenting Blacks in fiction between 1900 and 1940 when the "Harlem Renaissance" writers resisted the assumptions inherent in Black English dialect; and (6) reviewing Black English in American fiction which was published between 1945 and the present.

(018G) Kernan, Claudia M. Language Behavior in a Black Urban Community. Berkeley: University of California, Language-Behavior Research Laboratory, 1971.

The objective of this study is to determine the relationship of language variation to intra-cultural meaning in the Black community. Informants were working-class Blacks in Oakland, California. Kernan discusses: (1) select features which differentiate Black English from Standard English; (2) the attitudes of speakers of Black English; and (3) the social significance of such speech acts as signifying, marking and loud-talking.

(019G) Labov, William. Language in the Inner City: Studies in the Black English Vernacular. Philadelphia: University of Pennsylvania Press, 1972.

Using as observers white researchers who were linguists and Black researchers who were familiar with the culture of the inner-city Black community, this study's objective is to determine whether there are any connections among the Black venacular culture, linguistic skills, and success in reading by Black children. The informants were members of three Black street gangs in Harlem whose members ranged from 7 to 18 years. The findings indicated that there were no connections among linguistic-skills, the Black venacular culture and success in reading.

(020G) Luelsdorff, Philip A. A Segmental Phonology of Black English. The Hague: Mouton, 1975.

Data for this study was collected over a ten-year period. The principal informant was a fourteen year old male resident of Washington, D.C. The purpose of this study was to: (1) present a description of the segmental phonology of the Black English spoken by adolescents in Washington, D.C.: and (2) contribute to phonological and dialectological theory by specifying the ways in which Black English differs phonologically from standard English.

(021G) Mays, Luberta. Black Children's Perception of the Use of Dialect. Saratoga, Calif: R. & E. Pubs., 1977.

Mays focuses on the relationship between language patterns and reading achievement of Black second-graders. She: (1) identifies the Black child's perception of Black English as not the preferred speech; (2) examines the Black child's verbal quality of speech; and (3) discusses the relationship between dialect speech and the approach to the teaching of reading to Black children.

(022G) Smitherman, Geneva. Talkin' and Testyfying: The Language of Black America. Boston: Houghton Mifflin, 1977.

This important study critically discusses: (1) the history of Black English structure; (2) its present-day structure; (3) words and concepts in Black English; (4) the African and the Afro-American oral tradition; (5) Black modes of discourse; and (6) Black-white language attitudes. Its author proclaims that she seeks to answer the following questions: "Just what is Black English, where did it come from and what are the implications for black-white interactions and the teaching of Black children?"

(023G) Sutcliffe, David. British Black English. Oxford, England, New York: Blackwell, 1982.

The first part of this work is devoted to a discussion of the varieties of Black English spoken in Great Britian by Blacks and an analysis, using the works of Black writers in Great Britian, of the interaction between Black English and Black culture. Part II focuses on the theoretical linguistic aspects of British Black English.

(024G) Turner, Lorenzo Dow. Africanisms in the Gullah Dialect. Chicago: University of Chicago Press, 1949.

The Gullah dialect is a creolized form of English. It is spoken by a large number of Black Americans living in the coastal regions of South Carolina and Georgia. Some linguists believed that the Gullah dialect was derived from English dialects. In this classic study, Dr. Turner documents the similarities between the Gullah dialect and several West African languages. He records the most important Africanism in the Gullah dialect and cites their eqivalents in West African languages.

(025G) Twiggs, Robert D. Pan-African Languages in the Western Hemisphere PALWH [paelwh]: A Redefinition of Black Dialect as a Language and the Culture of Black Dialect. Quincy, Mass.: Christopher House, 1973.

Rejecting the term Black English, because of certain stated limitations, Twiggs proposes PALWH (Pan-African Language in the Western Hemisphere)

> "PALWH is a multi-language system derived in the Western Hemisphere transcending the geographical boundaries of English-speaking Africans - but the language spoken in the United States is still not Black English."

This volume, which is the first in a series to formalize Pan-African language in the Western Hemisphere, concentrates on Pan-African language and culture in the United States. Its fourteen chapters discuss the pronunciation and grammar of PALWH as well as the culture and grammar of PALWH from the pre-school level to the junior high school level. An extensive PALWH-English vocabulary is included in the appendix.

(026G) Vass, Winifred Kellersberger. The Bantu Speaking Heritage of the United States. Foreword by Baruch Elimelech. Los Angeles: Center for Afro-American Studies, University of California, Los Angeles, 1979.

Tshiluba is a Bantu language. In this study it is used as a basis for linguistic identification of Bantu speech survivals in the United States today. Among the topics discussed are: (1) the slave trade and its relationship to the Bantu speaking heritage; (2) Bantu place names in several southern states; and (3) Bantu speech survivals in Black American folktales.

(027G) Wolfram, Walt; Clarke, Nona H. Black-White Speech Relationships. Washington, D.C.: Center for Applied Linguistics, 1971.

The correlation between speech behavior and ethnicity is the topic of focus for the eight articles in this collection. The contributions, with publication dates spanning four decades, address several questions relative to the topic. Among some of them are: (1) In Black-White speech relations are there different influences on the speech of Blacks? (2) Is Black English derived from the creole languages spoken in the Caribbean Islands? and (3) Is Black English speech derived from southern white speech?

SELECTED JOURNAL ARTICLES

(028G) Loflin, M. D.; Guyette, T. "Impact of Education on Dialect Change." Linguistics No. 173 (May 23, 1976):49-62.

Lack of education, some linguists maintain, has resulted in archaic retentions by Blacks. This article explores the proposition that education does affect dialect change of Blacks, but only to a degree.

(029G) Okeke-Ezigbo E. "Paul Lawrence Dunbar: Straightening the Record." CLA Journal 24(June 1981):481-496.

Dunbar, Black literary critic Darwin Turner asserts, possessed a condescending attitude towards uneducated freedmen. Okeke-Ezigbo contends that this attitude "conditioned his stance on 'Negro dialect.' This facet of Dunbar's psychology as a poet is explored in this illuminating essay.

(030G) Cassidy, F. G. "Of Matters Lexicographical." American Speech 50(Spring/Summer 1975):87-89.

The word "Ofay" is the subject of this article. It is a term used by Black Americans among themselves to warn each other of the approach of a white man. Cassidy, in this article, traces the derivation of "Ofay" using dictionaries and the expertise of white and African linguists.

(031G) Hirshberg, Jeffrey. "Towards a Dictionary of Black American English on Historical Principles [with Glossary of Black American English on Historical Principals]" American Speech 57(Fall 1982):113-181.

Hirshberg outlines the editorial direction for a proposed "Dictionary on Black American English on Historical Principle." He proposes a dictionary which would allow for a systematic comparison of Black speech and white speech. As an example, he discusses the Dictionary of American Regional English, a project which is already in progress. This work, he observes, does "provide students of the language and culture of Black Americans with numerous examples of the Black idiom which have heretofore been undocumented."

(032G) Reed, Carol E. "Back to Square Two: Starting Over in the

1980s." Etc 39(Winter 1982):344-348.

The Language Curriculum Group was a research project based at Brooklyn College between 1970 and 1974. The primary and secondary goals of the project were to: (1) advance linguistic research on vernacular Black English spoken by inner-city Black and Hispanic students; (2) teach these students how to write college-level expository essays; (3) assist them in learning how to express themselves clearly; (4) educate teachers about the effects of dialect differences on students' writing; and (5) make teachers, curriculum planners and school administrators aware of the necessity of changing the methods used to teach students speaking vernacular Black English to write. In this published paper, which was delivered at the CUNY Association of Writing Supervisors at Hunter College in 1981, Reed describes in detail the Language Curriculum Group Projects.

(033G) Sebba, Mark. "Derivational Regularities in a Creole Lexicon: The Case of Sranan." Linguistics 19 No 1/2:101-117:1981.

In this article, Sebba discusses reduplication, compounding and multifunctionality used by speakers of Sranan to extend the language's lexicon.

(034G) Smith, William H. "Low-Country Black English." American Speech 54(Spring 1979):64-67.

The Low-Country is a strip of coastal land forty miles wide which extends from Georgetown, South Carolina, to the northeast corner of Florida. In one part of the Low-Country, the Sea Islands, Gullah, a creole language, is spoken by Blacks. This language has influenced Black speech throughout the United States. This article analyzes linguistically the speech patterns of three informants who lived in the Low-Country for eighty years or more. It focuses on such features as plural nouns, possessive pronouns, abjective nouns, present-tense verbs, past tense verbs and infinitives.

(035G) Spears, A. K. "Black English Semi-Auxiliary Come." Language 58(December 1982):850-872.

Two verbs of the shape "come" exist in Black English. This article discusses the motion verb "come" and the semi-auxiliary "come" as used in Black English.

(036G) Taylor, Clyde. "The Language of Hip: From Africa to What's Happening Now." First World 1(January/February 1977):25-32.

The language of the hip, the author declares

> "is not the same as Black English.
> It is an elitist lingo; within

Black English."

In this article the development of hip language among urban Blacks from the 1920s to the 1970s, as an expression of Black urban culture, is analyzed and discussed.

SELECTED DISSERTATIONS

(037G) Briggs, Cordell A. "A Study of Syntactic Variation in the Dialect Poetry of Paul Lawrence Dunbar." Ph.D. dissertation, Howard University, 1982.

Briggs provides a formal description of syntactic variation in Dunbar's dialect poetry. Dunbar's career is divided into three periods: "early years;" "middle years;" and "late years." Thirty-three poems from the three periods were selected for correlation. It was found that the poems produced during the "middle years" were most syntactically varied. Non-standard syntactical features of the poetry from this period were similar to the nonstandard syntactical features of Black English discussed today by such linguists as Fasald and Labov.

(038G) Craft, John A. "The Influence of Black Non-standard English on Person to Person Perception." Ph.D. dissertation, The University of Florida, 1981.

Many studies have concluded that speaker of stigmatized dialects of English are perceived less favorably than speakers of General American dialect. This study is designed to test whether speakers of the Black English dialect are perceived at a disadvantage when compared to speakers of General American dialect.

(039G) Dorrill, George T. "Black and White Speech in the South: Evidence from the Linguistic Atlas of the Middle and South Atlantic States." Ph.D. dissertation, University of South Carolina, 1982.

Utilizing materials in the Archives of the Linguistics Atlas of the Middle and South Atlantic States which are located at the University of South Carolina, Dorrill performs a phonological analysis of the speech of sixteen pairs of Black and white informants from Maryland (two pairs), Virginia (seven pairs), and North Carolina (seven pairs). The informants were interviewed between 1939 and 1940 and recorded in fine notation in field records. Dorrill's analysis is focused on the stressed vowel nuclei in English, because they are crucial phonological determinants for dialectical variation in American English.

(040G) Hansen, Renee Elsie. "Categorization Preference and Lexical Ambiguity Among Black Second Grade Children." Ph.D. dissertation, New York University, 1983. (440/07A,

p. 2136(44/07A, p. 2135).

To determine the relations among Black children of categorization preferences for the primary meanings of ambigious words, their knowledge of secondary meanings, and their understanding of secondary meanings is the subject of this study. Thirty-six Black second grade students of low socio-economic status attending public schools in metropolitan New York City were participants. The participants responded to Word Definition Tasks and Reading Comprehension Tasks. Hansen described the major findings in the following way:

> "The major finding revealed that categorization of primary meanings varied according to the individual word. Individual words and children's responses to those words were crucial factors."

(041G) Hudson, Barbara Hill. "A Descriptive Study of Male and Female Speech Stereotypes on Selected Television Shows with Predominately Black Characters." Ph.D. dissertation, Harvard University, 1982.

Based on theories from sociology, sociolinguistics and communications theory, this study analyzes the language used by male and female characters on two television shows: "The Jeffersons" and "Good Times." It examines differences in the language used in single and mixed sex conversations and differences in the language used by male and females. The main findings of this study indicated that there was a strong effect of race on all aspects of the study. White characters were consistently portrayed using a standard variety of English, whereas Blacks used a lesser standard variety of English.

(042G) Johnson, Gladys F. Dinkins. "Strengths of Selected Linguistic Features of the Oral Language Production of Young Advantaged Afro-American Children." Ed.D. Jackson State University, 1983.

Johnson identifies in this study selected features in the speaking language of advantaged Afro-American children. The informants are forty-eight third grade children attending public and parochial schools in the Metropolitan area of Central Mississippi from families with a median annual income of $16,553 or more and with one parent who had completed college. Speech samples and recorded interviews, in which responses from the informants were elicted by showing them a series of three stimulus pictures, were analyzed.

(043G) Reagan, Timothy Gerald "Language Ideology and Education: A Comparative Analysis of Bilingual Education Programs and the Question of Black English." Ph.D. dissertation, University of Selinais at Urbana-Champaign, 1982 (43/03A, p. 714).

The three disciplines of history, philosophy and linguistics are employed in this study to determine the best way for public schools to educate minority language speaking students. The history of minority language groups and the educational response to them from the Colonial period to the present is reviewed. An analysis of bilingual educational programs in the United States is presented. And, from the linguistic perspective, the nature of Black English and the problems Black English speakers posed in the Public schools are considered.

(044G) Stam, Yvonne G. "An Analysis of the Relationship Between Integrative Motivation and Standard English in Black Dialect-Speaking High School Students." Ed.D. Temple University, 1983.

Research studies on foreign students attending American universities have concluded that persons learn a second language when they want to become members of the group speaking that language. The Black dialect is the first language of many Black Americans. It deviates from Standard English to such a great extent that it might be viewed as a quasi-foreign language. Consequently, Standard English can be regarded as a second language to many Black Americans. The objective of this study is to examine whether "Integrative Motivation" is associated with the acquisition of Standard English by Black dialect-speaking high school students.

H. Ebony Visions in Color, Stone, Wood and Cloth: Afro-American Art

BIBLIOGRAPHIC WORKS

(001H) Davis, Lenwood; Sims, Janet L. Black Artists in the United States: An Annotated Bibliography of Books, Articles, and Dissertations on Black Artists, 1779-1979. Foreword by James E. Newton. Westport, CT: Greenwood Press, 1980.

Annotated citations on Afro-American art are presented in this conveniently arranged bibliography in six categories. They are: (1) major books on Black art; (2) general books which have significant chapters or sections on Black art; (3) major journal articles; (4) general articles in scholarly and popular magazines; (5) dissertations; (6) Black art works in the National Archives. The publication dates of the works cited are from the 1920s to the mid-1970s.

(002H) Holmes, Oakley N. The Complete Annotated Resource Guide to Black American Art. Spring Valley, N.Y.: Black Artists in America, C/O Macgowan Enterprises, 39 Wilshire Drive, Spring Valley, N.Y., 1979.

Containing citations to a potpourri of information on Afro-American art from the late 18th century to the mid-1970s, this work includes references to a variety of sources. Among some of them are: (1) books and dissertations; (2) exhibit catalogs; (3) prints; (4) motion pictures; (5) audio and video tapes; (6) art museums and galleries; and (7) professional lecturers.

(003H) Igoe, Lynn Moody. 250 Years of Afro-American Art: An Annotated Bibliography, by Lynn Moody Igoe with James Igoe. New York: Bowker, 1981.

Containing 25,000 citations to 3,900 Afro-American artists, this comprehensive annotated bibliography includes references not only to Afro-American artists but also artworks and art history. Citations are to books, periodicals, newspapers, exhibit catalogs, announcements, fliers, dissertations, theses, and such primary sources materials as diaries and letters. Although most references are to works published in English, there are citations to publications in Danish, Latin, Polish, Dutch, German, Spanish, French and Italian. Artists are included who are of African ancestry and who were born in the United States or who have worked as artists in this country. This work is divided into three sections: (1) "The Basic Bibliography"; (2) "The Subject Bibliography"; and (3) "The Artists Bibliography."

INDEXES

(004H) Chicago Public Library, W.P.A. Omnibus Project. Subject Index to Literature on Negro Art. Chicago: Chicago Public Library Omnibus Project, 1941.

Selected from the Chicago Afro-American Union Analytic Catalog, this annotated bibliography is composed of citations to Black art in the principal libraries of Chicago in the late 1930s. Of great value to the study of the history of Black art, this bibliography is arranged alphabetically by subject. The items included are monographs, parts of monographs, exhibit catalogs, and articles from domestic and foreign journals. Library locations are given for each citation.

(005H) Index to Black American Artists. Preface by Paxton Price. St. Louis: St. Louis Public Library, 1972.

Designed to aid students, teachers, and librarians researching in Black art, this is an index to books, periodical articles and exhibitions on Black art and artists. Arranged alphabetically by artist, each entry contains: (1) the name of the artist; (2) exhibits where the artist's work has been displayed; (3) medium; and (4) books and periodical articles having information on the artist or the artist's work.

CATALOGS OF SELECTED MAJOR ART EXHIBITIONS 1970-1984

(006H) Amistad II: Afro-American Art. Edited by David Driskell. [Exhibition] Nashville: Department of Art, Fisk University, 1975.

Exhibited in the Carl Van Vechten Art Gallery of Fisk University in 1975, "Armistad II: Afro-American Art" was a major exhibit of Afro-American art. The works of several outstanding Black artists, both living and deceased, were exhibited. Among them were: "Landscape," by Edward M. Bannister; "The Negro Boy," by Hale Woodruff; "Growing

Form," by Richard Hunt; "Christ at the Home of Mary and Martha," by Henry O. Tanner; "La Chaise Avex Fleurs," by Lois Jones Pierre-Noel; and "Baptizing in Oil," by Clementine Hunter. In addition to physical descriptions of all the works presented in the exhibition and photographic reproductions of some works, this catalog includes three important essays and commentaries related to the exhibition. They are: "The Amistad Incident," by Clifton Johnson; "Afro-American Art, An Inside View," by David Driskell; and "The Phenomenology of A Black Aesthetic," by Allen M. Gordon.

(007H) Boston Museum of Fine Arts. School of the Museum of Fine Arts. Afro-American Artists: New York and Boston. [exhibition at the Museum School in cooperation with the Museum of the National Center of Afro-American Artists and the Museum of Fine Arts, May 19-June 23, 1970]. Introduction by Edmund B. Gaither. Boston: The Museum School, 1970.

This exhibit, described as "one of the largest and most concentrated exhibitions of the works of contemporary Afro-American artists presented to the American Public," reflects new directions in Afro-American art in the late 1960s. Art historian/curator Edmund B. Gaither's "Introduction" is an informative historical commentary on Black art shows in America.

(008H) Driskell, David C. Two Centuries of Black Art. [exhibition] Los Angeles County Museum of Art, the High Museum of Art, Atlanta; Museum of Fine Arts, Dallas; the Brooklyn Museum. With catalog notes by Leonard Simon. [Los Angeles]: Los Angeles County Museum of Art. New York: distributed by Random House, 1976.

Containing 250 works of art by 78 Afro-American artists from the early 19th Century through the 1970s, "Two Centuries of Black American Art," sponsored by the Los Angeles County Museum of Art in 1976, was one of the largest exhibitions of Black American art assembled in the history of American art. First shown at the Los Angeles County Museum of Art, the exhibit was also displayed at: The High Museum of Art, Atlanta; The Museum of Fine Arts, Dallas; and the Brooklyn Museum. In this magnigicant catalog, Art Historian/Artist/ Art-educator, David Driskell's two-part illustrated, interpretive history of Black American art, "Black Artists and Craftsmen in the Formative Years, 1750-1920; The Evolution of a Black Aesthetic, 1920-1950," is a major treatise on the subject. Thirty-one color reproductions of various works in the Exhibit are presented in a section entitled "Color Plates." Leonard Simon's catalog notes include the following items on each artist: (1) name; (2) birthdate - deathdate; (3) brief biographical sketch; (4) titles of each work exhibited; (5) physical dimensions of the work; (6) date of the work's execution; (7) medium; (8) name of lender. In the case of anonymous works, the following items are cited: (1) title; (2) approximate date of execution; (3) medium; (4) place of execution; (5) physical description of the work;

(6) name of the lender. A selected bibliography on Black American art is included.

(009H) Forever Free: Art by African-American Women, 1862-1980. Arna Alexander Bontemps, Editor; Jacqueline Fonvielle-Bontemps, Director/Curator; David C. Driskell, Visiting Curator. Alexandria, VA: Stepheson; 1980.

The works of 40 Afro-American women artists were presented in this traveling historical exhibit. Included are works by Black women artists from 1862 to the late 1970s. Three essays in this catalog discuss authoritatively the role and critical significance of the artistic contributions of Black women in Afro-American art. They are: "Women As Artists in Sub-Saharan Africa," by Roslyn A. Walker; "African-American Art History: The Feminine Dimension," by Arna Alexander Bontemps and Jacqueline Fonvielle-Bontemps; and "A Critic's Viewpoint," by Keith A. Morrison.

(010H) Herbert F. Johnson Museum of Art. Cornell University. Directions in Afro-American Art. [exhibition], September 18 through October 27, 1974. Co-sponsored by the Africana Studies and Research Center, Cornell University. Ithaca, N.Y.: Cornell University, 1974.

The works of the 28 artists who were included in this exhibition, representing diverse directions in Afro-American art in the early 1970s, are described in this exhibit catalog. They are: Ralph Arnold; Kwasi Seitir Asantey; Ellsworth Ausby; David Phillip Bradford; Arthur Carraway; Leroy Clarke; Frederick J. Eversley; Leon N. Hicks; Suzanne Jackson; Wadsworth A. Jarrell; Marie Johnson; Benjamin Jones; Barbara J. Hones-Houg; Juan Logan; Phillip Lindsay Mason; Valerie Maynard; Geraldine McCullough; Bertrand Phillips; James Phillips; Leslie Kenneth Price; Raymond Saunders; Charles R. Searles; Alfred J. Smith, Jr.; Nelson Stevens; Russ Thompson; Leo Franklin Twiggs; Franklin White; and Jack White. Many of the artists submitted statements about their work. An extensive bibliography, including monographs, periodical articles and exhibit catalogs, is included.

(011H) Livingston, Jane; Beardsley, John. Black Folk Art in America, 1930-1980. With a contribution by Regina Perry. Jackson: University Press of Mississippi, 1982.

A catalogue of an exhibition held at the Corcoran Gallery of Arts in Washington, D.C., from January 15-March 28, 1982, this volume features the work of twenty Afro-American folk artists. They are: Jesse Aaron, Steve Ashby, Leslie Payne, Elyah Pierce, David Battle, Nellie Mae Rowe, Ulysses Davis, James 'Son Ford' Thomas, William Dawson, Mose Tolliver, Sam Doyle, Bell Traylor, William Edmondson, George White, James Hampton, George William, Sister Gertrude Morgan, Luster Willis, Inex Nathaniel, Joseph Yoakum. Regina Perry's essay, "Black American Folk Art: Origins and Early Manifestations" and John Beardsley's

"Spiritual Epics: The Voyage and the Vision in Black Folk Art"" are seminal, interpretive essays on Black folk art.

(012H) Museum of Fine Arts, Boston. Jubilee: Afro-American Artists on Afro-America. [exhibition] Museum of Fine Arts in Cooperation with the National Center of Afro-American Artists, 1977.

Portraying themes taken from Black music and poetry, this Bicentennial exhibition featured the works of Black artists which focused on Black rural and urban life for the last 75 years. The catalog, imaginatively written and designed by Edmund Barry Gaither, Director of the Museum of the National Center for Afro-American Artists, includes color and black/white reproductions which graphically illustrate the following themes: "Jubilee Folk"; "African Impressions"; "Night Life"; "All God's Children"; and "Struggle". Over 25 Black artists were represented in the exhibition.

(013H) Pippin, Horace. Horace Pippin. The Phillips Collection, Washington, D.C., February 25-March 27, 1977, Terry Dintenfass Gallery, New York, N.Y., April 5-30, 1977; Brandywine River Museum, Chadds Ford, PA, June 4-September 5, 1977. With an essay by Romare Bearden. Washington: [Phillips Collection], 1976.

The introductory essay to this catalogue by Pippin's friend and colleague, Romare Bearden, assesses Pippin's work and his contribution to American art. Forty-seven color reproductions of Pippin's work in chronological order of their creation are presented. A chronology of Horace Pippin's life and work is included from 1888 (year of birth) through 1976-77, his latest exhibition.

(014H) Ritual and Myth: A Survey of African American Art. [exhibition], the Studio Museum in Harlem, June 20-November 1, 1982. Text by Dr. Leslie King Hammond, guest curator. New York: Studio Museum, 1982.

With an illuminating introduction by artist/art historian, David Driskell, and a text and bibliography by Dr. Leslie King Hammond, this catalogue lists the works on display at the exhibition. These works are divided into the following categories: "African Art"; "The Academic Tradition"; "The Intuitives and Visionaries"; "The Caribbean"; "Contemporary Mythmakers".

(015H) Van Vechten Gallery. The Afro-American Collection, Fisk University, by David C. Driskell and Earl Hooks. Nashville: Department of Art, Fisk University, 1976.

Established in 1931, the Carl Van Vechten Art Gallery at Fisk University has developed into one of the major respositories of Afro-American and African art in the United States. In 1966, the Harmon Foundation augmented the Gallery's collection by giving some 400 paintings, drawings, prints, and sculpture by Afro-American and African artists to Fisk. Two years later, when the Harmon Foundation ceased, part of its extensive collection of Black art was also given to Fisk. This catalog lists and describes the items in the Carl Van Vechten Gallery.

(016H) Vlach, John M. The Afro-American Tradition in Decorative Arts. Cleveland: Cleveland Museum of Art, 1978.

In cooperation with the Links, Inc. of Cleveland, The Cleveland Museum of Art assembled a major exhibition on Afro-American folk art entitled "The Afro-American Tradition in Decorative Arts." This exhibition premiered at the Cleveland Museum of Art from February 1 through April 2, 1978. In subsequent months, it was a touring exhibit at major museums in Milwaukee, Birmingham, Boston, St. Louis, Seattle and Washington, D.C. Included in the Exhibit are outstanding and rare examples of basketry, musical instruments, woodcarving, quilting, pottery, bootbuilding, blacksmithing, architecture, and graveyard decoration. These artifacts are from many personal and private collections. This volume is the exhibition and illustrations of many of the artifacts, an excellent commentary of Afro-American folk arts, notes on all of the exhibit items, and an extensive bibliography.

(017H) Van Vechten Gallery. The Rites of Color and Form. [Exhibition of] paintings, prints, ceramics, sculpture, by Earl Hooks and David C. Driskell. Nashville: Carl Van Vechten Gallery, Fisk University, 1974.

This catalogue describes items in the 45th Annual Arts Exhibition held April 21-May 17, 1974 at the Van Vechten Gallery which featured the works of David Driskell and Earl J. Hooks. Biographies of both artists are included.

SELECTED TREATISES

(018H) Biggers, John; Simms, Carroll. Black Art in Houston: The Texas Southern University Experience. With John Edward Weems. Introduction by Donald Weismann. College Station: Texas A & M University Press, 1978.

Artists John Biggers and Carroll Simms organized in the late 1940s the Art Departmant at Texas Southern University in Houston. In this work, biographical sketches are presented on both artists/teachers. Numerous reproductions of their works and the works of their students constitute the major part of the volume.

(019H) Dover, Cedric. American Negro Art. [Greenwich, Conn.]: New York Graphic Soceity, 1960.

Containing numerous color and black/white reproductions of

the major works of Black artists and artisians from the late eighteenth century to the late 1950s, this is an illustrated history of the art of Black America with a interpretive commentary. An extensive bibliography on Black art and a thumbnail - biographical sketch/index to artists whose works are included in the volume makes it a valuable source.

(020H) Ferris, William, ed. Afro American Folk Art and Crafts. Boston: G. K. Hall, 1983.

In this collection of nineteen essays, interviews, commentaries and histories, writers explore various facets of Afro-American folk art. William Ferris' introductory essay sets the tone of the collection by suggesting the psychological roots of Black Folk Art. Contributions by the seventeen other writers discuss artists and techniques in seven types of Black folk art: (1) quilt makers; (2) sculptors; (3) instrument makers; (4) basketmakers; (5) builders; (6) blacksmiths; and (7) potters.

(021H) Fine, Elsa H. The Afro-American Artist: A Search for Identity. New York: Holt, Rinehart and Winston, 1973.

Covering the years from the late 18th century to theearly 1970s, Fine interprets the Black visual artist's attempt to express his identity through his work. This volume is well-illustrated with color and black/white photographs and reproductions.

(022H) Lewis, Samella S. Art: African-American. New York: Harcourt, Brace, Jovanovich, 1978.

Citing the political, social and economic forces which influenced the growth of Black art in America, Lewis traces its development. She divides the history of Black American art into six periods from 1619 to the mid 1970s. Within each period, the contributions and significance of major Black artists are discussed and interpreted. An extensive bibliography of books, exhibit catalogs and periodical articles is included.

(023H) Porter, James A. Modern Negro Art. New York: Dryden Press, 1943.

This scholarly classic history of Black art in America spans the years from the mid-eighteenth century through the early 1940s. Porter explores the development of fine art, the decorative arts as well as folk art and graphic arts among Afro-Americans.

(024H) Locke, Alain LeRoy. Negro Art: Past and Present. Washington, D.C.: Associates in Negro Folk Education, 1936.

Locke's classic work discusses the history of Black art in America and Africa. His discussion, with numerous illustrations, is confined primarily to the fine arts. Each item included is annotated.

(025H) Murray, Freeman H. H. Emancipation and the Freed in American Sculpture. Washington: Murray Brothers Printing Co., 1916.

This volume is one of the earliest extensive studies to consider seriously the works of Black sculptors. It is a critique of the works of Black and white sculptors who used Black Americans as their subjects.

(026H) The Other Slaves: Mechanics, Artisians, and Craftsmen. edited by James E. Newton and Ronald Lewis. Boston: G. K. Hall, 1978.

Slave artisians, mechanics and craftsmen have made significant contributions toward the development of American architecture, woodworking, ironwork, and other decorative arts. In this collection of nineteen essays and articles the plight and artistry of slave artisians, mechanics and craftsmen are discussed. These writings are grouped under three headings: "Part I - Skilled Slaves: The Industrial Impact; Part II - Slave miners and Mechanics; Part III - Slave Artisians and Craftsmen." A directory of occupations held by Black artisians prior to 1865 is included in the appendix.

(027H) Thompson, Robert F. Flash and Spirit: African and Afro-American Art and Philosophy. New York: Random, 1984.

This work discusses the rise, development and achievements of Yowba, Kongo, Fon, Mande, and Eagham art and philosophy and their fusion with New World art and aesthetics. In examining this fusion, Thompson defines the Black-Atlantic visual art tradition.

BIOGRAPHICAL WORKS

(028H) Afro-American Artist: A Bio-bibliographical Directory. Compiled and edited by Theresa Dickason Cederholm. Boston: Trustees of the Boston Public Library, 1973.

Spanning the years from the slave craftsmen of the 18th century to the artists of the early 1970s, this work is a directory to Black artists and artisians, their works, exhibits and literature about them. Arranged alphabetically by the artist or artisan, each entry includes the following items: (1) artistic media of the artist/artisan; (2) vocation; (3) birth date and place; (4) education; (5) titles of works; (6) date and place of exhibits; (7) collections where works are housed; (8) awards; (9) professional memberships; (10) agents or professional representatives; (11) biographical sources.

(029H) Atkinson, J. Edward, comp. Black Dimensions in Contemporary Art. New York: New American Library, 1971.

Edward S. Spriggs, Executive Director, The Studio Museum of Harlem, in his preface to this book, describes it in the following terms:

> "This collection presents the forms and styles operative in the works or artists who have been assembled together, not because their creations are related by styles or form of some kind of school, but because they happen to be Afro-American or artists of African descent. This is a visual survey."

Forty-nine Black American artists, their works, and philosophies of Black art are presented in this volume.

(030H) Fax, Elton. Black Artists of the New Generation. Foreword by Romare Bearden. New York: Dodd, Mead, 1977.

In this collective biography, Fax interviews 17 young Black American artists from various parts of the United States. The artists discuss their personal: (1) motivations for becoming artists; (2) philosophies of Black aesthetics; (3) views of Black art; and (4) artistic goals. The 17 artists are Maurice Burns, Shirley Stark, Alfred Hinton, Carole Byard, Bertrand Phillips, Valerie Maynard, Kermit Oliver, Trudel Obey, Otto Neals, Kay Brown, Alfred Smith, Jr., Onnie Millar Manuel Gomez, Mirian B. Frances, Emory Douglas, Rosalind Jefferies, John Outterbridge, Horathel Hall, and Dana Chandler.

(031H) Ferris, William. Local Color: A Sense of Place in Folk Art. Edited by Brenda McCallum. With a foreword by Robert Penn Warren. Developed by the Center for Southern Folklore. New York: McGraw-Hill, 1982.

In the rural South, Black and white folk artists share many close bonds. They both regard the past with reverence and they have a "sense of place." Utilizing taped interviews, William Ferris presents illuminating, intimate and illustrated autobiographical/biographical commentaries on nine Black and white folk artists in Mississippi. They are: Victor "Hickory Stick Vic" Babb, Cane Maker, Vicksburg; Leon "Peck" Clark, Basket Maker, Sharon; Louis Dotson, One-string Guitar Maker, Lorman; Theora Hamblett, Painter, Oxford; Ethel Wright Mohamed, Needleworker, Belzoni; James "Son Ford" Thomas, Sculptor, Leland; Othar Turner, Cane Fife Maker, Senatobia; Pecolia Warner, Quilt Maker, Yazoo City; Luster Willis, Painter and Cane Maker, Terry.

(032H) Fuller, Edmund L. Visions in Stone: The Sculpture of William Edmondson. Philadelphia: University of Pittsburg, 1973.

In 1931, when William Edmondson, a Black Nashvillian(Tenn.), retired from his job as a janitor in a Nashville establishment, he began "...to cut away on some stone" in reaction to a vision he claimed that he had from God. Examples of Edmondson's stonecutting soon dotted many graveyards in Nashville and caught the attention of the art world. Including 108 plates of Edmondson's work, this volume assesses the Black stonecutter's sculpture and its place in American art.

(033H) Lewis, Samella. The Art of Elizabeth Catlett. Claremont, CA: Hancraft, 1984.

Elizabeth Catlett has come to the realization that art must be a liberating force for Black people. In this work, Lewis examines the work and life of Catlett, one the geniuses of Black American art.

(034H) Lewis, Samella S.; Waddy, Ruth G. Black Artists on Art. Vols. 1 & 2. Los Angeles: Contemporary Crafts, 1969, 1971.

In this unique two-volume work, Black artists present their philosophical views on Black aesthetics in art. Photographs of each artist and reproductions of their work accompany their philosophical statements. A brief biographical sketch of each artist appears in the appendix.

(035H) Mathews, Marcia. Henry Ossawa Tanner. Chicago: University of Chicago Press, 1969.

Based on his personal papers, this factual account of Tanner's life details the artist's young life in Pittsburgh through his years as a struggling artist in the United States and, later, Paris. Mathews chroncicles Tanner's successes as artist abroad and his eventual recognition in the United States.

(036H) Parks, James D. Robert S. Duncanson: 19th Century Black Romantic Painter. Washington: Associated Publishers, 1980.

Robert S. Duncanson was one of the finest, but neglected, American landscape painters of the first sixty years of the nineteenth century. Born in Mr. Healthy, Ohio, of mixed parentage, Duncanson studied for a period in Scotland, where he was influenced by the writings of William Shakespeare, Sir Walter Scott, and Alfred Lord Tennyson. His paintings were exhibited in Scotland, England, Italy and Canada. Before the Civil War, he was commissioned to paint murals by Nicholas Longworth for his mansion in Cincinnati which is known today as the Charles P. Taft Museum. In 1972, the Cincinnati Art Museum presented an exhibition entitled: "Robert S. Duncanson - A Centennial Exhibition." Artist/ Art Historian/Art Educator, James Dallas Parks, in this biography, presents many little known facts about this pioneer Black nineteenth century painter.

SELECTED JOURNAL ARTICLES

(037H) "Black Artists of Los Angeles: Conversations with 5 Black Artists." Studio Potter. 9(June 1981): 16-25.

Five Black Los Angeles artists are skillfully interviewed in this article. They are: Stanley Charles Wilson; Doyle Lane; Nathaniel Bustian; Marsha Johnson; and Doyle Brockman Davis.

(038H) Calo, Mary Ann, "Winslow Homer's Visits to Virginia During Reconstruction." American Art Journal. 12(Winter 1980): 4-27.

Along with Thomas Eakins and William Sidney Mount, Winslow Homer's treatment of Black Americans in portraiture has been heralded as original and sensitive. This substantive commentary critically assesses Homer's Black portraiture which resulted from his travels in Virginia during the Reconstruction Period.

(039H) Metcalf, E. W. "Black Art, Folk Art, and Social Control." Winterthur Port. 18(Winter 1983): 271-89.

In this enlightening essay Metcalf discusses the changing role of Black folk art as a measure of social control among Blacks.

(040H) Ransaw, Lee A. "Changing Relationship of the Black Visual Artist to His Community." Black Art 3(No. 3): 44-56.

During the Black Revolution of the 1960s, Black artists experienced a dramatic change in their relationship with the Black community. Leaders of the Black community set up guidelines for the content of Black art. Black art was to serve the Black nation functionally and psychologically. In this article, Ransaw explores the nature of the changing relationship between the Black artist and his community.

(041H) Sims, Lowery S. "Bob Colescott Ain't Just Misbehavin" Artforum. 26(March 1984): 56-9.

The use of Black stereotypes in Bob Colescott's transpositions of masterpieces of American art has evoked much criticism from the art world and Black political leaders. Lowery S. Sims' article discusses Colescott's artistic objectives and the impact of several of his works.

(042H) Tate, Mae. "Suzanne Jackson." Black Art. v. 4: 3-21.

Black California artist and poet, Suzanne Jackson, is profiled in this extensive article. Author Tate describes the artist's youth in California and Alaska, presents several reproductions of her work, and assesses her contributions as an artist and poet.

(043H) Wilson, Judith. "Myths and Memories: Bob Thompson." Art in America. 71(May 1983): 139-43.

Born in Louisville, in 1937, Bob Thompson emerged as one of the leading young Black artists in the late 1950s, painting in the Abstract-Expressionist mode. Judith Wilson discusses Thompson's career and assesses his contributions to American art before he died on Memorial Day in 1966.

SELECTED DISSERTATIONS

(044H) Campbell, Mary Schmidt. "Romare Bearden: A Creative Mythology." Ph.D. dissertation, Syracuse University, 1982.

Romare Bearden's search for mystic vision which permitted him to create universal art without losing his individual indentity is the subject of this study. Utilizing the chronological approach, Campbell examines several significant periods in the artist's life. They include: his childhood and youth in Charlotte, North Carolina, and Harlem during the Harlem Renaissance; the years he worked as a WPA artist; his years with the Koatz Art Gallery during which time he was influenced by Abstract Expressionism; and the later years during which he engaged in water colors and oils using cubist vocabulary, and relied on classical western literary texts.

(045H) Fox, James E. "Inconography of the Black in American Art (1700-1900)" Ph.D. dissertation, Columbia University, 1979.

Black Americans have been the minor and mjor subjects in the works of white American artists since the early 18th century. The study traces the attitudes of white Americans toward Black Americans as reflected in the works of white American artists from 1710 through 1900.

(046H) Gordon, Allan. "Cultural Dualism on the Themes of Certain Afro-American Artists." Ph.D. dissertation, Ohio University, 1969.

Every Afro-American creative artist experiences cultural duality. Allan Gordon, in this classically significant study, examines the phenomenon of cultural duality as reflected in the themes embodied in the works of Black visual and literary artists Jacob Lawrence, Charles White, Hughie Lee-Smith, Eldzier Cortor, Leroi Jones, Langston Hughes, Melvin B. Tolson, and Richard Wright.

I.
Jazz, Spirituals, Blues and Gospel: Black Music

BIBLIOGRAPHIES

(001I) DeLerma, Dominique-Rene. Bibliography of Black Music. Westport, CT: Greenwood Press, 191-84.

This four-volume work is one of the most extensive bibliographies to appear on Black music. All entries, however, are unannotated. The titles of individual volumes are: Bibliography of Black Music, Volume 1: Reference Materials; Bibliography of Black Music, Volume 2: Afro-American Idioms; Bibliography of Black Music, Volume 3: Geographical Studies; Bibliography of Black Music, Volume 4: Theory, Education, and Related Studies.

(002I) Floyd, Samuel A., Jr.; Reisser, Marsha J. Black Music in the United States: An Annotated Bibliography of Selected Reference and Research Materials. Millwood, New York: Kraus International Publications, 1983.

Designed for undergraduates as well as experienced researchers this carefully compiled bibliography includes seventeen types of research and reference materials on Black music. They are: general guides; dictionary catalogues and related sources; bibliographies of bibliographies; discographies and catalogues of sound recordings; indexes and guides to periodical literature; dictionaries and encyclopedias; general Black music histories, chronologies, and cultural studies; topical studies; collective biographies; iconographies; pedagogy; periodicals; anthologies and collections of printed music; records and record collections; repositories and archives. Title, author and subject indexes greatly enhance the value of this splendid work.

(003I) Jackson, Irene V., Comp. Afro-American Religious Music: A Bibliography and a Catalogue of Gospel Music. Westport, CT: Greenwood Press, 1979.

Citations to 873 works on or related to the development of

Black religious music in the United States, the Caribbean and West Africa are contained in this unannotated bibliography. Its second section is devoted to a catalogue of Black Gospel compositions in the Library of Congress between 1938 and 1965.

(004I) Skowronski, Jo Ann. Black Music in America: A Bibliography. Metuchen, NJ: Scarecrow Press, 1981.

Containing unannotated citations to books and articles in journals, this bibliography includes references on Black music and musicians in the United States from the Colonial Period through 1979. Excluded are musical compositions, phonograph records, films, and newspaper articles. The work is divided into three sections: "I. Selected Musicians and Singers; II. General References; III. Reference Works." It is indexed by author and all 14,319 citations are numbered consecutively.

(005I) Tischler, Alice. Fifteen Black American Composers: A Bibliography of Their Works. Detroit: Information Coordinators, 1981.

Biographical sketches and citations to the compositions of fifteen Black composers of "Art Music" are included in this work. "Art Music" is defined by Tischler as:

> "A particular type of music meant especially for the concert stage, dramatic media, or church, distinguishing it from such of types as popular music, jazz, and folk music with their many subgroupings."

The fifteen Black American composers are: Edward Boatner; Margaret Bonds; Edgar Clark; Arthur Cunningham; William Dawson; Roger Dickerson; James Furman; Adolphus Hailstork; Roger Harris; Wendell Logan; Carman Moore; Dorothy Moore; John Price; Noah Ryder; Frederick Tillis.

(006I) White, Evelyn D. Choral Music by Afro-American Composers. Metuchen, NJ: Scarecrow Press, 1981.

This bibliography was compiled specifically for choral conductors with the hope that they will include more compositions by Black composers in their choral repetoire. Arranged alphabetically by composers with titles listed alphabetically under the composer, each entry contains the following items: (1) title of the composition; (2) number of pages; (3) voicing and solo requirements; (4) vocal ranges; (5) range of difficulty; (6) a capella; (7) type of accompaniment; (8) publisher; and (9) catalog number, if available.

DISCOGRAPHIES

(007I) The Chess Label: A Discography. Compiled by Michel Ruppli. Westport, CT: Greenwood Press, 1983. 2v.

From 1947 to 1971 many top name Black jazz, blues and Gospel artists recorded on the Chess Label. Among some of them were Chuck Berry, Bo Diddley, Kenny Burrell, Etta James, the Salem Travelers and the Soul Stirrers. This discography of Chess recordings is divided into four parts. Part I is a listing of sessions of original Chess masters between 1947 and 1971. Part II is a listing of GRT sessions made from 1971 and 1975 after GRT had purchased Chess in 1971. Part III lists singles recorded on Aristocrat, Checker, Chess, Martarry, Cadet and Cadet Concept labels. Part IV lists album recordings.

(008I) Tudor, Dean; Tudor, Nancy. Black Music. Littleton, Col.: Libraries Unlimited, 1979.

A survey and buying guide to Black music on long-playing recordings and tapes, this discography is designed for librarians and individuals attempting to build sound recording collections of Black music. Annotations of 300 words have been written for approximately 1,300 long-playing recordings and tapes which were in print in 1978-79. Selections are arranged under the following subject headings: Blues, Rhythm 'N' Blues; Gospel; Soul; Reggae.

(009I) Turner, Patricia. Afro-American Singers: An Index and Preliminary Discography of Long-Playing Recordings of Opera, Choral Music, and Song. Minneapolis: Challenge Productions, 1977.

Focusing on Afro-American singers whose careers have been as performing artists on the concert stage, this index and discography presents essential information on the lives and recording activities of over 100 Afro-American singers. The main entries, arranged alphabetically by singer in a section entitled "Singers and Recordings," list the following items: (1) name of singer; (2) type of voice; (3) brief biographical sketch; (4) selected quotations from record reviews; (5) citations to long-playing recordings by the singer; and (6) selected biographical sources. Other types of entries are arranged under four groups: (1) choral groups; (2) composers and recordings; (3) arias; and (4) songs.

YEARBOOKS

(010I) Black Music Research Journal, 1984. Chicago: Black Music

Research Center, Columbia College, 1984-

This yearbook, which was published by The Fisk University Institute for Research in Black Music (1980-83), is presently published by the Black Music Research Center of Columbia College. Its annual articles continue to represent some of the foremost research conducted in Black music. The following articles appear in this volume of the yearbook: "Prejudice Lives: Toward A Philosophy of Black Music Biography," by Bruce Tucker; "The Sources and Resources of Classic Ragtime Music," by Samuel A. Floyd, Jr. and Marsha J. Reisser; and "A Concordance of Scores and Recordings of Music by Black Composers," by Dominique-Rene De Lerma.

SEMINAR PROCEEDINGS

(011I) Black Music in Our Culture; Curricula Ideas on the Subjects, Materials and Problems, by Dominique-Rene De Lerma, with contributions from Thomas Jefferson Anderson, Jr. and others. Kent, OH: Kent State University Press, 1970.

This work is based on a seminar entitled "Black Music in College and University Curricula" which was held at Indiana University from June 18 to June 21, 1969. The papers and interviews presented explore Black music in the music curricula in high school and college.

TREATISES

(012I) Abdul, Raul. Blacks in Classical Music: A Personal History. New York: Dodd, Mead, 1977.

Since the mid-nineteenth century Black Americans have distinguished themselves in various aspects of classical music. Among some of these early pioneers were: Elizabeth Taylor-Greenfield (1819-1876), the outstanding concert soprano who was known as the "Black Swan"; Justin Holland (1819-1886) who wrote two standard guitar manuals; and the concert pianist Thomas Green Bethune (1849-1908), commonly knows as "Blind Tom." This work documents the achievements of Black Americans in classical music in seven areas: composers; singers; opera and operas companies; keyboard artists,; instrumentalists; conductors, orchestras, and chrouses; divertisements; and critics.

(013I) Berlin, Edward A. Ragtime: A Musical and Cultural History. Berkeley: University of California Press, 1980.

In this comprehensive history of Ragtime, Berline reviews the origins and early history of Ragtime focusing of how this music was received by audiences. Part Two is devoted to detailed discussion of Piano Ragtime. In an appendix is included a location index for Piano Rags in selected anthologies.

(014I) Brooks, Telford. America's Black Musical Heritage. Englewood Cliffs, NJ: Prentice-Hall, Inc., 1984.

Each genre of Afro-American music is discussed from the historical and present-day perspective in a section of this volume. The compositions of major composers in the genre are analyzed and an extensive discography of their works is presented.

(015I) Dennison, Sam. Scandalize My Name: Black Imagery in American Popular Music. New York: Garland Publishing Co., 1981.

Selecting a sample of 4,000 titles of sheet music in which Black subjects were manifested or implied, Dennison attempts in this study to analyze the use of Black imagery in throughout the history of American music. The titles selected are popular music. Dennison asserts: "The purpose of this study is to investigate racism as it appears in our popular songs on the Black Subject."

(016I) Epstein, Dena J. Sinful Tunes and Spirituals: Black Folk Music to the Civil War. Urbana: University of Illinois, 1977.

Based on an examination of Colonial, Antebellum, and Civil War literature, Epstein in this survey documents the development of Afro-American folk music in Africa and the United States from the late 18th century to 1865. Her investigation includes secular as well as sacred Black folk music.

(017I) Handy, D. Antoinette. The International Sweethearts of Rhythms. Metuchen, NJ: Scarecrow Press, 1983.

The International Sweethearts of Rhythm was an extraordinary all-female band which was organized in the late 1930s by Laurence Clifton Jones, President of Piney Woods Country Life School in Piney Woods, Mississippi, to raise funds for the school. Because of the exceptional talent of many of the members of the International Sweethearts of Rhythm, the band gained national recognition and toured, between 1937 and 1941, throughout the United States. In 1941, the International Sweethearts of Rhythm turned professional. Dr. Handy, in this well-researched volume, documents the musical activities of this unusual musical organization.

(018I) Lovell, John. Black Song: The Forge and the Flame; the Story of How the Afro-American Spiritual was Hammered Out. New York: Macmillan, 1972.

This masterful work on the Afro-American Spiritual is divided into three parts. "Part One: The Forge" focuses on the origin, range and definition of the Spiritual. "Part Two: The Slave Sings Free" discusses the Spiritual as part of Afro-American folk Music." Part III: The Flame" explains how the Spiritual has become a world phenomenon.

(019I) McKee, Margaret. Beale Black and Blue: Life and Music on Black America's Main Street, by Margaret McKee and Fred Chisenhall. Baton Rouge: Louisiana State University Press, 1981.

This is a well-documented history of Memphis' famous Beale Street and its musicians. Part I is a discussion of Beale Street's history from the late nineteenth century to the 1970s. Each Chapter in Part II is devoted to interviews with the following Beale Street musicians: Furry; Booker; Piano Red; Big Mama; Sleepy John and Hammie; The Honey-dripper; The Mississippi Sheik; Big Joe; Big Boy; Upcountry; B. B. Bobby; and Big Albert.

(020I) Oakley, Giles. The Devil's Music: A History of the Blues. New York: Taplinger, 1977.

This social history parallels the development of the Blues with the history of Black people in America. It is well documented and contains many rare photographs of Blues events and Blues performers.

(021I) Ricks, George R. Some Aspects of the Religious Music of the United States Negro: An Ethnomusicological Study with Special Emphasis on the Gospel Tradition. New York: Arno Press, 1977.

Originally written as a dissertation at Northwestern University, this anthropological study analyzes the historical-cultural forces which have influenced the development of Afro-American religious music, particularly Gospel music, from the pre-Civil War period to the 1950s. Ricks employed field and library research to complete this broad-based study.

(022I) Schafer, William J.; Riedel Johannes. The Art of Ragtime: Form and Meaning of an Original Black American Art. Baton Rouge: Louisiana State University Press, 1973.

Ragtime was the first type of music created by Black Americans to achieve commercial success. This study analyzes the form and structure of Ragtime. It focuses on aspects as Classic Ragtime; Ragtime songs and Ragtime Bands; and Ragtime style and performance.

(023I) Southern, Eileen. The Music of Black Americans. 2nd Edition. New York: Norton, 1984.

Undoubtedly the most comprehensive history of Black music to appear to date, this work documents in detail all forms of Afro-American musical activity from 1619 to the late 1970s. An extensive bibliography and sicography accompanies each chapter.

(024I) Travis, Dempsey J. Autobiography of Black Jazz. Chicago: Urban Research Institute, 1983.

In this sprawling volume, Travis discusses the development of jazz in the Black community of Chicago from the late nineteenth century through the early 1980s. An important feature of this work is the short autobiographies of twenty-six jazz musicians and entertainers.

(025I) Trotter, James M. Music and Some Highly Musical People. Boston: Lee and Shepard, 1880 (reprinted by Chicago: Afro-Am Press, 1969).

Published in 1880, this classic work was one of the earliest histories to appear on American music and was the first history on Afro-American music. After discussing the nature, history and aesthetics of music, Trotter presents biographical sketches of numerous nineteenth century Afro-American Musicians and commentaries on some Afro-American musical organizations such as The Fisk Jubilee Singers; The Colored American Opera Company, and Frank Johnson and His famous Military Band and Orchestra.

COLLECTIVE BIOGRAPHICAL WORKS

(026I) Berry, Lemuel. Biographical Dictionary of Black Musicians and Music Educators. Guthrie, OK: Educational Book Pubs., 1978.

Biographical sketches of Black composers, musicians, conductors, educators, singers, instrumentalists, publishers, scholars, directors, musicologists and music critics are included in this directory which spans the years from the late 1800s to the present. The seventeen appendices provide a variety of information about Black music and musicians such as lists of professional choirs and small ensembles, Gospel organizations, and minstrel companies.

(027I) The Black Composer Speaks. Edited by David N. Baker, Lida Belt and Herman C. Hudson. A Project of the Afro-American Arts Institute, Indiana University. Metuchen, NJ: Scarecrow Press, 1978.

Black composers have been neglected by the American musical establishment, although their works have been performed by many of the nation's most prominent musical organizations. In this volume, the authors present interviews of fifteen

Black composers and catalogues of their works. The composers are: Thomas Jefferson Anderson; David Nathaniel Baker; Noel Da Costa; Talib Rasul Kakim; Herbie Hancock; Ulysses Kay; Undine Smith Moore; Oliver Nelson; Coleridge-Taylor Perkinson; George Russell; Archie Shepp; Hale Smith; Howard Swanson; George Walker; Olly Wilson.

(028I) Handy, D. Antoinette. Black Women in American Bands and Orchestras. Metuchen, NJ: Scarecrow Press, Inc., 1981.

As members of orchestras and bands, Black women have made significant contributions to the development of Afro-American music. Lillian Hardin Armstron, for example, as a member of "King Oliver's legendary Creole Jazz Band," greatly influenced the style of another member of that band, Louis Armstrong. Alice McLeod Coltrane, playing with John Coltrane's outfit, is said to have greatly enhanced the performance of that group. Handy, after discussing the historical development of bands in America, presents well-research biographical sketches of Black women who were members of bands and orchestras.

(029I) Pearson, Barry Lee. "Sounds So Good to Me." The Bluesman's Story. Philadelphia: University of Pennsylvania Press, 1984.

A host of Blues artists, the majority of whom are Black and from the South, present their life stories as Blues musicians through skillfully conducted interviews. The interviewees are: Sam Chatmon, Lee Crisp; Jimmy Dawkins, David "Honeyboy" Edwards; Fred McDowell; Clyde Maxwell; Yank Rachel; Otis Rush; Johnny Shines; Sunnyland Slim; Byther Smith; Roosevelt Sykes; Eddie Taylor; James Thomas; Big Joe Williams; Johnny Young' Wild Child Butler; Big Chief Ellis; Bob Lowery; Joe Cephas; Archie Edwards; John Jackson; J. T. Adams.

(030I) Southern, Eileen. Biographical Dictionary of Afro-American and African Musicians. Westport, CT: Greenwood Press, 1982.

Including biographical sketches of more than 1,500 musicians of African descent, this comprehensive dictionary presents sketches for musicians who were born, with some exceptions, between 1642 and 1945. Information on the following items are presented: (1) name of the musician; (2) musical occupation; (3) dates and places of birth and death; (4) career details; (5) bibliographical and discographical sources.

PERIODICAL ARTICLES

(031I) "An Oral History: The Great Lakes Experience," with notes by Samuel Floyd. The Black Perspective in Music 2(Spring 1983)41-61.

During World War II more than 5,000 Black musicians were recruited into the United States Navy and trained at Great Lakes Naval Training Station, near Chicago, as bandsmen. After a period of training, these musicians were dispersed in twenty-five piece units throughout the United States and overseas. Three of the units, including some of the finest Black musicians, remained at Great Lakes. This article is a transcript of a group-interview conducted with these musicians in 1976 by Professor Samuel Floyd, Dr. London Branch, and Dr. Warrick Carter. The interviewees are: Len Bowden, Thomas Bridges, Howard Funderburt, Major Holley, Huel Perkins, Charles Pillars, Hayes Pillars, Clark Terry, Rufus Tucker, Ernie Wilkins, Jimmy Wilkins and Mitchell ("Booty") Wood.

(032I) Boyer, Horace C. "Charles Albert Findley: Progenitor of Black-American Gospel Music." The Black Perspective in Music. 2(Fall 1983):103-132.

Charles Albert Findley was one of the originators of Gospel music. In 1921 he published the first Gospel hymnal for use in the Black church, The Gospel Pearls. Dr. Boyer in this article, originally presented as a peper at The Colloquium on Charles A. Findley at the Smithosonian Institute, 7-9 May, 1982, reviews the musical career of Findley as a composer, focusing of his significant role in the development of Gospel music.

(033I) Burden, James Revel. "Conversation with...Joe Turner: Last of the Stride Pianists." The Black Perspective in Music 9(Fall 1981):183-192.

Joe Turner was once introduced by Oscar Peterson as the "World's Greatest Stride Pianist." Turner, who has been playing a style called "stride piano" for over sixty years has spent the last thirty years in Europe entertaining. In this interview, he comments on the early years of his career, his assessment of other jazz artists, and his own musical philosophy.

(034I) Edwards, Vernon H.: Mark, Michael L. "In Retrospect: Clarence Cameron White." The Black Perspective in Music 9(Spring 1981):51-72.

Clarence Cameron White achieved international fame as a violinist, conductor and composer. This article details White's musical accomplishments such as the performance of his opera, "Ouanga," by the American Opera Society of Chicago in 1932 and White's "String Quartet in E Minor" performed at the Ecole Normale de Musigne in Paris in 1931.

(035I) Gover, R. M. "Opera Ebony's Artistic Landmarks: Their

Contribution to History." Opera Quarterly, Vol 2 (No. 2, 1984):57-68.

Between 1873 and 1970, at least seven opera companies were founded by Afro-Americans: The Colored American Opera Company (1873); Drury Grand Opera Company (1900); Aeolian Opera Associates (1934); The Detroit Negro Opera Company (1938); The National Negro Opera Company (1941); and The Dra-Mu Opera Company (1960). With the exception of the Detroit Negro Opera Company, currently known as the Detroit Civic Opera Company, all of these opera companies folded. In 1972 Benjamin Matthews, a well-known bass baritone; Wayne Sanders, a successful pianist; Margaret Harris, the well-known Black female conductor; and Sister Mary Elsie, a retired nun and college professor who had organized the Xavier University Grand Opera Company, founded Opera Ebony. Based in Philadelphia, this highly successful Afro-American opera company presented performances which have won high praise from critics in New York and Philadelphia. Ruth Gover, in this article, details the triumphs and struggles of Opera Ebony since its founding.

(036I) Headlee, Judith Ann Stills. "Willaim Grant Still: A Voice High-Sounding" (includes transcription of a 1968 taped interview). Music Educators Journal 70(February 1984):24-30.

In 1968, R. Donald Brown of California State University taped several interviews with Black composer/conductor William G. Still. The tapes were almost forgotten in the files of the California State University's Oral History Department until 1978 when Still passed. An instructor, Shirley Stevenson, brought them to the attention of the Still Family. Judith Anne Still Headlee, Still's daughter, and his widow transcribed the tapes and returned them to California State University. In this article, Headlee presents sections of the interview. Among the subjects which Still discusses are: (1) his collegiate years at Wilberforce and Oberlin; (2) his early work as an arranger; and (3) his work as a conductor with the Los Angeles Philharmonic Orchestra.

(037I) Spencer, Jon Michael. "R. Nathaniel Det's Views on the Preservation of Black Music." The Black Perspective in Music. 10(Fall 1982):133-148.

Dett's concern that Spirituals would be lost to posterity is discussed in the article. Dett gave three reasons for this concern: (1) the indifference of Americans to things of native origin and the great admiration by American Musicians for European ideals; (2) the scarcity of literary masterpieces on Negro themes; and (3) the lack of proper musical and academic training among Negro composers.

(038I) Stephens, Robert W. "Soul: A Historical Reconstruction of Continuity and Change in Black Popular Music." The Black Perspective in Music 12(Fall 1984):21-43.

The collective sensibilities of the Black community are reflected in soul music. Stephens examines the musical phenomenon of Soul music by discussing its: (1) evolution; (2) relationship to historical and socio-political events; and (3) musical character and dissemination through emergent musical styles.

(039I) Stewart, James B. "Perspectives on Black Families from Contemporary Soul Music: The Case of Millie Jackson." Phylon 25(March 1980):57-71.

Because of the shortage of Black men, many Black women are forced to share their men. This concept of sharing a love mate is the theme of two albums by Black vocalist Millie Jackson: "Caught Up" and "Still Caught Up." In this article, Stewart analyzes the songs in these albums as a social commentary on Black life.

SELECTED DISSERTATIONS

(040I) Burnim, Mellonee V. "The Gospel Music Tradition: Symbol of Ethnicity." Ph.D. dissertation, Indiana University, 1980.

Burnim identifies concepts in Black Gospel music which regulate it as a vehicle of expression for Blacks of any religious affiliation. The congregations of two Black churches are used as research populations. This study analyzes the meaning and significance of Gospel music by examining an actual performance event and conducting feedback interviews, using a videorecording of the musical event, to elicit comments and criticisms from the interviewee.

(041I) Carter, Nathan M. "Samuel Coleridge-Taylor: His Life and Works." D.M.A. dissertation, Peabody Institute of Johns Hopkins University, 1984.

Samuel Coleridge-Taylor, the celebrated Afro-English composer, wrote 82 works with opus numbers and several songs before he died at the age of 37 in 1912. This study is the first to examine his musical style by a modern scholar. It covers his life, discusses his professional activities and analyzes his works.

(042I) Dargan, William T. "Congregational Gospel Songs in a Black Holiness Church: A Musical and Textual Analysis." Ph.D. dissertation, Wesleyan University, 1983.

A body of songs regularly sung by the congregation of a Black holiness church are analyzed in this study to determine the relationship between musical forms and textual themes. It was found that what was termed as Type V harmonic patterns appeared in texts about struggle. Texts conveying conflict were generally associated with Type VI harmonic patterns. Ascending terraced melodic were most often found in texts which expressed praise.

(043I) Davidson, Celia E. "Operas by Afro-American Composers: A Critical Survey and Analysis of Selected Works." Ph.D. dissertation, Catholic University of America, 1980.

Eight operas by six Afro-American Composers are analyzed and discussed in this study. The composers and their operas are: (1) Harry Lawrence Freeman (1869-1954), "The Martyr" (1893), "Vendetta" (1923), and "Voodoo" (1923); Scott Joplin (1868-1917), "Treemonisha" (1911); Clarence Cameron White (1880-1960), "Ouanga" (1923); William Grant Still (1895-1978), "Highway I, U.S.A." (1962); Mark Fax (1911-1974), "A Christmas Miracle"; Ulysses Kay (1917) "Jubilee."

(044I) Estill, Ann H. M. "The Contributions of Selected Afro-American Women Classical Singers: 1850-1955." D. A. dissertation, New York University, 1982.

The careers and contributions of five Afro-American classical women singers are discussed in the study. They are Elizabeth Taylor-Greenfield, Sissieretta Jones, Marie Selika, Lillian Evanti and Mattiwilda Dobbs. These artists' careers span the years from 1850 to 1955.

(045I) Porter, Lewis. "John Coltrane's Music of 1960 through 1967: Jazz Improvisation as Composition." Ph.D. dissertation, Brandeis University, 1983.

John Coltrane's musical style is the subject of this study. It focuses on his control of long range structure during improvisation. In addition to examining the saxaphone styles of Coltrane and other saxaphonists during the 1950s and 1960s, Porter also analyzes three key pieces by Coltrane, "Equinox," "A Love Supreme," and "Venus."

(046I) Thomas, Andre Jerome. "A Study of the Selected Masses of Twentieth Century Black Composers: Margaret Bonds, Robert Ray, George Walker, and David Baker." D. M. A. dissertertation, University of Illinois at Champaign-Urbana, 1983.

Four twentieth century Black composers who have written Masses are discussed in this study. Each chapter, devoted to one composer, presents: (1) a biographical sketch of the composer; (2) a detailed discussion of pertinent details of the Mass, such as its premiere performance, publication, recordings, reviews, and an analysis of its structure and composition; and (3) a description of production problems. In an appendix is included a listing of Mass compositions by other twentieth century Black composers.

(047I) Tyler, Mary A. L. "The Music of Charles Henry Pace and Its Relationship to the Afro-American Church Experience." Ph.D. dissertation, University of Pittsburgh, 1980.

Charles Henry Pace was a prolific Black composer/arranger of church and secular music. He composed 104 original church songs, 8 spiritual medleys and arranged 45 Spirituals. Pace was, also, an outstanding choral director. Many of the characteristics in Pace's published religious songs are found in Afro-American Church music today such as parallel harmonies, intervallic undulations and voice glides. In this study, the published religious songs of Charles Henry Pace are analyzed in an effort to determine their relationship to the Afro-American Church experience.

J.
Shadows in the Wings: Blacks in the Performing Arts

DIRECTORIES AND COLLECTIVE BIOGRAPHIES

(001J) Bogle, Donald. Brown Sugar: Eighty Years of America's Black Female Superstars. Designed by Joan Peckolick. New York: Harmony Books, 1980.

Highlights of the professional careers of important Black female performing artists who were active between 1900 and 1980 are presented in this collective biography. Each biography is illustrated with publicity photographs of the biographee.

(002J) Mapp, Edward. Directory of Blacks in the Performing Arts. Metuchen, NJ: Scarecrow, 1978.

This directory to more than 850 living and deceased Black performers embraces every spectrum of the performing arts such as dance, film, music, radio, television, and the theatre. Arranged alphabetically by biographee, each entry contains the following information: name of the performer; birthdate/death date (when deceased); education; address; medium; career data; membership; publications; performances; and relatives in the performing arts.

(003J) Mitchell, Loften. Voices of the Black Theatre. Clifton, NJ: James T. White and Co., 1975.

Eight outstanding Black performers present recollections of their experiences in the theatre in this unique collective autobiographical work. These personal reflections are prefaced with an introductory essay and ended with an epilogue by Loften Mitchell. The eight performers are: Ruby Dee, Abron Hill, Eddie Hunter, Paul Robeson, Dick Campbell, Vinnette Carroll, Frederick O'Neal, and Regina Andrews.

DRAMA

Bibliographies

(004J) Afro-American Poetry and Drama, 1760-1975: A Guide to Information Sources. Detroit: Gale Research Co., 1979.

This two-part work contains unannotated bibliographies to Afro-American poetry and drama. Part one which is entitled Afro-American Poetry, 1760-1975, by William P. French, Michel J. Fabre, and Amrityit Singh, lists citations to Afro-American poetry in general studies and to the poetry of individual poets from 1760 through 1975. Part two, Afro-American Drama, 1850-1975, by Genevieve E. Fabre, includes citations to bibliographies, play collections, critical studies, and individual dramatists.

(005J) Arata, Esther Spring. Black American Playwrights, 1800 to the Present: A Bibliography, by Esther Spring Arata and Nicholas John Rotali. Metuchen, NJ: Scarecrow Press, 1976.

Over 1,550 plays dated from 1800 by 530 Black playwrights are cited in this three-part bibliography. Part one is an alphabetical listing of Black playwrights and their plays with citations to criticisms, reviews and awards, Part two is a selected bibliography. Part three is title index to plays in part one.

(006J) Arata, Esther Spring. More Black American Playwrights: A Bibliography, by Esther Spring Arata. With the Assistance of Marlene J. Erickson, Sandra Dewitz, Mary Linse Alexander, Metuchen, NJ: Scarecrow Press, 1978.

Including citations to articles in periodicals and newspapers as well as books, this bibliography contains entries spanning the years from 1970 to 1978. Approximately 490 Black playwrights, and white playwrights who collaborated with Black playwrights, are included in this volume, of which 190 appeared in the 1976 edition. Section one is a alphabetical listing of playwrights, their works, with citations to criticisms and reviews of their works, and awards. Section two is a general bibliography. Section three is an index to play titles.

Dictionaries

(007J) Woll, Allen. Dictionary of the Black Theatre: Broadway, Off-Broadway, Selected Harlem Theatre. Westport, CT: Greenwood Press, 1983.

Treatises and Essays

(008J) Craig, E. Quita. Black Drama of the Federal Theatre Era: Beyond the Formal Horizons. Amhurst: The University of Massachusetts Press, 1980.

From 1935 to 1939, the WPA-sponsored Federal Theatre Project flourished under the direction of Hallie Flanagan. In addition to providing employment to theatrical personnel and producing first-rate dramatic productions for millions of Americans, The Federal Theatre Project provided unprecedented opportunities for the growth of Black playwrights and Black drama. Basing her research on the Federal Theatre Project archives, which were uncovered in an airplane hangar in Baltimore in 1974, E. Quinta Craig discusses the theatrical productions and activities Black playwright and theatre personnel who worked on The Federal Theatre Projects such as Hughes Allison, Theodore Ward and others. Her analysis of the works of Federal Black playwrights includes such topics as "The duality of Black drama," the "transformation of Stereotypes," and "The West Indian influence."

(009J) Fabre, Genevieve. Drumbeats, Masks, and Metaphor: Contemporary Afro-American Theatre. Translated from the French by Melvin Dixon. Cambridge: Harvard University Press, 1983.

The Black Theatre has had a distinguished history. At its center has been the objective to establish a sense of Black identity in all Black people. Fabre discusses what she perceives to be the stages of development in The Black Theatre. She examines and discusses the destinctive elements which characterized The Black Theatre prior to the 1960s; the revolutionary purpose of "The Militant Theatre" as exemplified by the plays of Le Roi Jones/Amiri Baraka; and the focus on the Black life experience in "The Theatre of Experience" as illustrated in the dramas of Ed Bullins, J. E. Gaines and Melvin Van Peebles.

(010J) Harrison, Paul L. The Drama of Nommo. New York: Grove Press, Inc., 1972.

Nommo means "word force." The drama of Nommo evokes in Black people a communal sense of their spirituality. Harrison observes:

> "The theater is charged, then, with the responsibility of revealing the necessary light that might refocus the community's moral universe to re-establish the order found in the vigor of our communal tradition."

Harrison explores in this illuminating study the phenomenon

of Nommo Force in the drama of the revolutionary Black theatre.

(011J) Hill, Errol. Shakespeare in Sable: A History of Black Shakespearean Actors. Amherst: University of Massachusetts Press, 1984.

Black actors have always exhibited an enthusiasm for playing Shakespearean roles. In 1821, James Hewlit became the first Black American Shakespearean actor, playing the leading role in the "Richard III" production of the African Company, the first Black theatrical company established in the United States. Errol Hill, in this well-researched volume, documents and discusses Black actors and actresses who have played Shakespearean roles, focusing on their successes, hardships and reception by the public.

(012J) Hill, Errol, ed. Theatre of Black Americans. New York: Prentice-Hall, 1980, 2v.

What is the Black Theatre? Does the Black Theatre of today have historical antecedents? What cultural and political objectives does the contemporary Black Theatre attempt to achieve? These and other questions are discussed in this two-volume work of 28 essays. Among the contributions included are: "Notes on Ritual in the New Black Theatre," by Shelby Steele; "Shuffle Along: keynote of the Harlem Renaissance," by Helen Armstead Johnson; "Mom, Dad and God: Values in Black Theatre," by William Cook; "The Lafayette Players, 1917-1932," by Sister Francesca Thompson, O.S.F.; "The Negro Ensemble Company; Report and Reflections: A Transcedent Vision," by Ellen Foreman; "The Black Theatre Alliance," by Thomas D. Pawley; and "Critics, Standards and The Black Theatre," by Margaret B. Wilkerson.

(013J) King, Woodie, Jr. Black Theatre: Present Condition. New York: National Black Theatre Touring Circuit, 1981.

Based on his personal experiences and observations, theatrical producer Woodie King, Jr. gives a candid appraisal of the state of the Black Theatre in America. King's commentary embraces such subjects as racism in the American Theatre; the movement by Blacks to start their own theatre; and the theft of Black art by white Americans.

(014J) Isaacs, Edith J. R. The Negro in the American Theatre. College Park, MD: McGrath Publishing Co., 1968 (first published 1947).

This classic history of the Afro-American in the American theatre traces its growth for the 1820s to the late 1940s. Although not a scholarly study, the work is a good illustrated general history of Blacks in the

American theatre.

(015J) Mitchell, Loften. Black Drama: The Story of the American Negro in the Theatre. New York: Hawthorn Books, 1967.

Mitchell documents the theatrical activities of Black Americans and the development of Black drama in New York City from 1776 to the mid-1960s in the light of prevailing and changing social, economic, political and social forces. Highlighted in this study are the significant contributions of major Black playwrights, performers, producers, and critics whose contributions not only influenced the development of Black drama but are still changing the attitudes of white Americans towards Black performers and Black drama.

(016J) Sandle, Floyd L. The Negro in the American Theatre: An Organizational Development, 1911-1964. [Grambling, LA:] N.P. 1964.

The growth and development of speech and drama departments and theatrical productions on the campuses of historically Black colleges and universities between 1911 and 1964 are discussed in this study. Sandle focuses on the history of Black Americans in the commercial theatre; persons who played significant roles in the development of "The Little Theatre" at historically Black colleges and universities; and the Southern Association of Dramatic and Speech Arts, an organization which promoted dramatics at historically Black colleges and universities.

MOTION PICTURES

Bibliographies and Filmographies

(017J) Hyatt, Marshall, ed. The Afro-American Cinematic Experience: An Annotated Bibliography and Filmography. Wilmington, DE: Scholarly Resources, Inc., 1983.

Containing an annotated bibliography and a filmography, this work is an adequate reference tool for researching the Afro-American in motion pictures. The annotated bibliography, arranged alphabetically by author and title, contains citations to books and articles in periodicals on Black films. The filmography, which includes major films in the Afro-American cinematic experience from 1915 to the present, is arranged alphabetically by film title. Each entry presents the following items: title of the film; producer; director; members of the cast; and an annotation. In a second section of the filmography, films are classified in 10 categories such as "Black Independent Films"; "Blaxploitation Films"; and "Documentaries." An index to the annotated bibliography is included.

(018J) Klotman, Phyllis R. Frame by Frame - A Black Filmography. Bloomington: Indiana University Press, 1979.

This comprehensive compendium contains over 3,000 films and film items with Black themes or subject matter, or Blacks participating substantially as actors, writers, producers, musicians, animators, consultants, or walk-ons. Films and film items which are included were produced from 1900 through 1977 in the United States, Mexico, Central America, South America, the Carribean, and sub-Sahara Africa. The following items are presented in each entry: (1) film title/series title; (2) narrator/cast; (3) writer; (4) producer; (5) director; (6) studio/company; (7) technical information; (8) date/country of origin; (9) type; (10) distributor/archive; and (11) brief annotation. Five indexes provide access to the filmography by Black performers, author, screenplay writer, producer, and director.

Treatises and Essays

(019J) Archer, Leonard C. Black Images in the American Theatre: NAACP Protest Campaigns - Stage, Screen, Radio and Television. Brooklyn, NY: Pageant Poseidon, 1973.

In 1915 the NAACP launched a nationwide campaign, protesting the film "Birth of a Nation," because Black leaders believed the film presented a distorted image of Black Americans during the Reconstruction Period. This study reviews and analyzes the protest campaigns of the NAACP and other organizations from 1915 through the 1970s to protest: (1) the dehumanizing image presented of the Afro-American in the theatre, motion pictures, radio and television; and (2) the lack of employment opportunities for Black Americans in these industries.

(020J) Bogle, Donald. Toms, Coons, Mulattoes, Mammies: An Interpretive History of Blacks in American Films. New York: Viking, 1973.

The changing roles of Black Americans in fictional films are analyzed in this unique study. Bogle examines fictional films in which Blacks were actors from "Cooning and the Wedding of a Coon" (1905) to "Shaft" (1971).

(021J) Cripps, Thomas. Black Film as Genre. Bloomington: Indiana University, 1978.

An excellent overview discussing Black genre films from the 1920s to ABC-TV's "Roots" is presented in this study. Six Black genre films are analyzed in depth: a social drama; a religious film; a Black documentary, a Blaxplortation film; a musical; and a Black pastoral film. Cripps histography of Black film greatly enhances the reference value of this study.

(022J) Cripps, Thomas. <u>Slow Fade to Black: The Negro in American Film</u>, 1940-1942. New York: Oxford University Press, 1977.

1942 was a watershed year for Black Americans in the motion picture industry. Delegates from the NAACP and the heads of Hollywood's major studios met and agreed on some social changes and procedures to improve the treatment of Black Americans in films and the film industry. This historic meeting marked the beginning of the end of the struggle by Black Americans for equal treatment in the American film industry. Thomas Cripps in this study traces the involvement of Black Americans in the motion picture industry from 1900 to 1942 from the perspective of changing economic, political, and social forces which shaped the industry during these years.

(023J) Leab, Daniel J. <u>From Sambo to Superspade: The Black Experience in Motion Pictures</u>. Boston: Houghton, Mifflin, 1975.

Focusing on the characterization of Blacks in films from 1900 through the early 1970s, this study traces the evaluation of Black characterization from the docile, happy-go-lucky, and slow-witted Rastus in "Rastus in Zululand" (1910) to the indestructible, flippant and romantic John Shaft in "Shaft" (1971). Leab concludes that both characterizations of Blacks are dehumanizing.

(024J) Maynard, Richard A. <u>The Black Man on Film: Racial Stereotyping</u>. Rochell Park, NJ: Hayden Book Co., 1974.

Throughout its history, the motion picture industry has released films portraying Blacks in stereotype images. This collection of essays is intended to be a resource book to accompany the viewing of motion pictures which have presented Blacks as stereotypes. These writings are grouped under six topics which chronologically consider the historical phases of Black stereotyping in films. They are: "Anything But a Man - A Historical Survey of the Black Stereotype on Film, 'Birth of A Nation'; Stepin Fetchin to Carmen Jones'-Some Samples of Opinion (1929-1955); A 'New' Image for the Future?; Beyond Sidney Portier - Possible Solutions and Trends for the Future; The Movie Indian and the Movie Jew - Parallel studies in Stereotyping." A filmography of films portraying Black stereotypes is included.

(025J) Nesteby, James R. <u>Black Images in American Films, Eighteen Ninety-Six to Nineteen Fifty-Four: The Interplay Between Civil Rights and Film Culture</u>. Washington: University Press of America, 1982.

In this enlightening study, the history of the Black American in motion pictures is analyzed in the light of his struggle to gain civil rights. Nestby covers the years from the Plessy vs Brown decision of 1896 to the late 1970s.

(026J) Sampson, Henry T. Blacks in Black and White: A Source Book on Black Films. Metuchen, NJ: Scarecrow Press, 1977.

The Black motion picture industry from 1910 to 1950 is analyzed and discussed in this study. After presenting a historical overview of Black-cast film production from 1910 to 1950, Sampson focuses on: the Lincoln Motion Picture Company; The Micheauz Film Corporation and Oscar Micheaux; white independent film companies which produced Black-cast films; and Black independent film companies. Synopses of some all-Black films produced between 1910 and 1950 are presented. Three useful appendices are included which cite all-Black films produced from 1904 through 1950; give a partial listing of individuals and corporations that produced films from 1910 to 1950; and film credits for featured players in Black-cast films, 1910-1950.

(027J) Yearwood, Gladstone. Black Cinema Aesthetics: Issues in Independent Black Filmmaking. Athens: Ohio University, Center for Afro-American Studies, 1983.

This collection of nine essays explores aesthetic principles for a Black cinema as opposed to Black-oriented cinema, which characterizes most Black films produced in Hollywood today. These contributions, discussing various aspects of the subject are: "New Black Cinema and Uses of the Past," by Thomas Cripps; "Afro-American Literature As A cultural Resource for a Black Cinema Aesthetic," by Vattel T. Rose; "Sex Imagery and Black Women in American Cinema," by Pearl Bowser; "'Sweet, Sweetback's Baadassss Song' and the Development of the Contemporary Black Film Movement" and "Toward A Theory of A Black Cinema Aesthetic," by Gladstone L. Yearwood; "The Politics of African Cinema," by Harold Weaver; "The Development of the Contemporary Black Film Movement," by St. Clair Bourne; "On Independent Black Cinema," by Hailo Gerima; "Cultural Restitution and Independent Black Cinema." by Tony Gittens.

DANCE

Treatises

(028J) Aschenbrenner, Joyce. Katherine Dunham: Reflections on the Social and Political Context of American Dance. New York: CORD, 1981.

Katherine Dunham was an artistic innovator and pioneer in modern dance whose influence on the development of American dance was equal to that of the triumvirate of Martha Graham, Doris Humphreys and Charles Weidman. Yet, her contributions, because of racism and her protest activities against segregation, have not become a substantive part of American dance history. Joyce Aschenbrenner assesses Dunham's impact on the development of Black dance, modern dance and the teaching of modern dance in America. The Dunham Teaching Method is documented in this study with excerpts from the diary of Lavinia Williams, a professional Black dancer and former student of Katherine Dunham in the 1940s.

(029J) Cayou, Delores Kirton. Modern Jazz Dance. Palo Alto, CA: National Press Books, 1971.

Two aspects of Modern Jazz Dance are presented in this work. In the opening chapter Cayou discusses its historical development from dance in African culture to contemporary social and stage dance, highlighting its influence on minstrel shows, vaudeville and Black dance, in general, in the United States. The remaining chapters are devoted to: warm-up exercises; rhythmic exercises and sequences, isolations; turns; walks and combinations; class planning; and music.

(030J) Emery, Lynne F. Black Dance in the United States from 1619 to 1970. With foreward by Katherine Dunham. New York: Dance Horizons, 1980.

The first comprehensive study on Black dance, this work traces the development of Black dance from the years of the slave trade to the concert stage of the United States in 1970. Emery organizes this narrative around chronological periods in the history of Black dance such as the slave trade, dance in the Carribean from 1518 to 1900; dance on the plantations during slavery; dance in minstrelsy after the Civil War; and dance in the theatre and dance hall between 1900 and 1930. From 1930 through 1970 only Black dance on the concert stage is discussed.

(031J) Ka so! Katherine Dunham: An Anthology of Writings. Edited by Ve'Ve' A. Clark and Margaret B. Wilkerson. Berkeley: University of California, Institute for the Study of Social Change-CCEW Women's Center, 1978.

Katherine Dunham laid the groundwork for great Black dance through the choreographers' performances and anthogiological studies on Haitian dance. In 1976, when Katherine Dunham was a visiting professor at the University of California - Berkeley. The Ka so! Textile Exhibit was opened in her honor. This volume, including the program opening the exhibit, in an anthology of writings by and about Katherine Dunham.

SELECTED PERIODICAL ARTICLES

(032J) Andrews, W. D. E. "Theatre of Black Reality: The Blues Drama of Ed Bullins." Southwest Review. 65(Spring 1980): 178-90.

The plays of Ed Bullins, unlike the drama of Amiri Baraka which advocates revolutionary changes in the lives of Blacks, examine Black life and forces Blacks to see themselves as they really are. Both playwrights, leaders in the American Black Arts Movement and responding to the Black activist challenge, directed their plays to Black audiences. Andrews analyzes two of Bullins plays in terms of his aesthetics of the blues. The two plays are: Clara's Ole Man (1965); In New England Winter (1967).

(033J) Bailey, A. Peter. "Alvia Ailey at the Met." Ebony. 39(October 1984):164-6 .

Founded by Texas-born Alvin Ailey, in 1959, The Alvin Ailey American Dance Theatre celebrated its 25th anniversary in 1974 with a precedent-setting two-week engagement on the stage of the Metropolitan Opera House in New York. A. Peter Bailey in this beautifully illustrated article recounts the successes and misfortunes which the dance comapny has experienced. Although finance is a major problem facing the company, Bailey cites another.

> "The other is more subtle and possibly more insidious. Some elements in the dance world appear to be very resentful of the company's artistic success. They often try to put the company down as 'too commercial'"

Such a criticism, Bailey concludes, can hurt the company's fundraising efforts.

(034J) Bygrave, Mike. "A Soldier's Story." Sight and Sound. 54(Winter 1984/85):17-19.

The directors, actors, crew members, and publicists of the film, A Soldiers Story, air their views in this article on the plight of the Black actor, racial self-hatred among Blacks, and the reception of the film. All agree that A Soldier's Story is not a "Black Film." But the film's actors express various viewpoints on the role of the Black actor in society.

(035J) Cripps, Thomas. "Movies, Race, and World World II: Tennessee Johnson as an Anticipation of the Strategies of the Civil Rights Movement." Prologue.

14(Summer 1982):49-67.

During World War II, the stage was set for postwar civil rights strategies by Black activists, liberal whites and government agencies who jointly advocated the concept of promoting the philosophy of victory over the axis forces abroad and victory over racism at Rome. One of these government agencies was The Office of War Information and its Hollywood Branch. Through the efforts of this agency's officers, several of the major motion picture companies were prodded into producing documentaries describing the positive involvement of Black Americans in the war effort. In this prize-winning essay, Thomas Cripps discusses the activities on the motion picture industry on behalf of Black Americans during World War II, focusing on the role played by Tennessee Johnson.

(036J) Dempsey, Michael; Gupta, Udayan. "Hollywood's Color Problem." American Film. 7(April 1982):66-70.

Charging a decline in the number of Blacks employed in the motion picture industry in the early 1980s, NAACP leaders threaten a massive boycott of the movies. Using statistics from various sources, statements from motion picture industry executives and NAACP officials, Dempsey and Gupta investigate the alleged charges.

(037J) Desmond, Jane. "African Dance: A Southerner Brings It Home." Southern Exposure. 12(July/August 1984): 35-8.

Chuck Davis, Director of the nationally-recognized Chuck Davis Dance Company of New York, returned to his native North Carolina in 1983 to establish his second African-American dance company: The African-American Dance Ensemble. Based in Durham, this new dance company, which is integrated, gave its first professional concert in February, 1984. Author Jane Desmond profiles the dynamic Chuck Davis and describes the successful first year of their unique southern African-American dance company.

(038J) Graustark, Barbara. "Tapped for Stardom: Gregory Hines, the Toast of Broadway Steps Into the Hollywood Spotlight." American Film. 10(December 1984):28-32+.

Before going to Hollywood, Gregory Hines had achieved success on Broadway. His dancing won him Tony Award nominations for "Eubie!", "Comin' Uptown." and "Sophisticated Ladies." Hines the man and his blooming career are profiled in this article which describes his relationships with colleagues and his roles in the films "The Cotton Club" and "White Night."

(039J) Gwynne, James B. "Marie Brooks Dance Theatre: Leading the Children to Dance." Dance Magazine. 56(August 1982): 46-7.

In 1973 dancer/choreographer Marie Brooks founded in New York City, the children's Dance Research Theatre presently named the Marie Brooks Dance Theatre. The artistic objective of the program of this unique dance organization is to teach Black children between the ages of 8 and 18 Black dance by instructing them in the cultural and historical "meaning" of dance movements used in African and Carribbean dances. James B. Gwynne describes the components of the Theatre's program and reports on the benefits realized by its students.

(040J) Harris, Davis. "The Original 'Four Saints in Three Acts.'" Drama Review. 26(Spring 1982):101-130.

In the late 1920s, Gertrude Stein and Virgil Thomson combined their talents to write an avant-garde opera, "Four Saints in Three Acts.' The opera premeired in Hartford, Connecticut at the theatre of the Wadsworth Athenaeum, Hartford's art museum, in 1934, with novice production artists and an all-Black cast. Variety, in one of its 1934 editions, claimed that the opera had gotten more media space than any other production of the season. This article describes the circumstances surrounding the premiere performance of Four Saints in Three Acts, the production staff, and the all-Black cast.

(041J) Leff, L. J. "David Selznick's Gone With the Wind: the Negro Problem." The Georgia Review. 38(Spring 1984): 146-64.

In the late 1930s, when David Selznick was in the early stages of planning the production of Gone with the Wind several groups inside and outside of the film community expressed critical concern that the finished film would not treat the Afro-American objectively. The Production Code Administration, the NAACP, and the Black Press appealed to Selznick to project a favorable image of the Afro-American in his film-rendering of Margaret Mitchell's book. This article describes the agitating activities of these groups between 1936 and 1939, when "Gone with the Wind" was finally viewed by the American public.

(042J) Richards, Sandra L. "Negative Forces and Positive Non-Entities: Images of Women in the Dramas of Amiri Baraka." Theatre Journal. 34(May 1982):233-40.

Richards observes that there are three types of images of women found in Amiri Baraka's plays.

> "...the evil white woman who is aggressively independent of everyone; the neurotic black woman who consciously wills her own destruction and the black or white woman who is a paragon of political virtue."

This article examines these three images of women projected by Baraka in his plays.

(043J) Sanders, Charles L. "Debbie Allen." Ebony. 38(March 1983):74-6.

Debbie Allen, as the dancing instructor in the television series "Fame," is profiled in this article. Sanders discusses her domestic life, professional career, and her immediate family.

(044J) Schiff, Ellen. "Inside of the Outsider: Blacks and Jews in Contemporary Drama." Massachusetts Review. 21(Winter 1980):801-12.

Traditionally in American drama the Jew and the Black have been assigned by most white dramatists to roles and images which have defined them as "outsiders" in American life. Contemporary Black and Jewish dramatists, accepting this convention, have inverted this traditional stereotype of Black and Jews in their plays. For example, a Jew in one Black dramatist's play is not presented as the traditional crafty, wicked businessman but as a poor, ill-advised real estage agent. A Jewish playwirght, for instance, has created a Black college-bound youth with vision and compassion, not as the stereotyped dutiful menial Black. In this article, Ellen Schiff explores this kind of characterization in the plays of several contemporary Black and Jewish playwrights.

SELECTED DISSERTATIONS

(045J) Abookire, Noerena. "Children's Theatre Activities at Karamu House in Cleveland, Ohio, 1915-1975." Ph.D. dissertation, New York University, 1982.

The Children's Theatre of Cleveland's famed Karamu House has received national and international acclaim for its precedent-making theatrical productions and related activities. This study describes the work of ten directors of The Children's Theatre between 1915 and 1975, including the innovative and creative directing efforts of founder Rowena Jeliffe and Ann K. Flagg. For this study, Abookire utilizes personal interviews with several directors, the Jeliffe collection and written questionnaires.

(046J) Ashton, Charlotte R. "The Changing Image of Blacks in American Film: 1944-1973." Ph.D. dissertation, Princeton University, 1981.

Between 1944 and 1973, drastic changes occurred in the political, social and economic life of the United States which affected the status of the Afro-American. The civil rights movement focused the eyes of the country on the Afro-American's struggle for equality. This study attempts to determine whether or not there was a significant and positive change in the image of the Afro-American projected in the motion pictures produced during these years.

(047J) Gill, Glenda E. "Six Black Performers in Relation to the Federal Theatre." Ph.D. dissertation, The University of Iowa, 1981.

Black performers have always faced discrimination in securing serious dramatic roles. There was, for example, a separate booking system: The Theatre Owners Booking Association. From 1935 to 1939 WPA's Federal Theatre Project (FTP) sought to combat discriminatory practices against Black performers. In this study, the careers of five Black performers who were associated with the FTP are described in contrast to the career of one Black performer who was not associated with FTP. The five performers are Canada Lee, Edna Thomas, Rex Ingram, Thomas C. Anderson, and Arthur Dooley Wilson. The career of Ethel Waters, who was not associated with FTP, is compared with the careers of the five FTP performers.

(048J) Hazzard-Piankhi, Maisha L. A. "Black Love on Stage: A Profile of Courtship and Marriage Relationships in Selected Broadway Shows by Black Dramatists, 1959-1979, and An Original Play." Ph.D. dissertation, Bowling Green State University, 1983.

Seven plays by Black dramatists which were produced on Broadway between 1959 and 1979 and one play by Maisha L. A. Hazzard-Piankhi. "Awake When Its Evening," are analyzed in an effort to describe courtship and marriage relationships in contemporary Black drama. These relationships are discussed in terms of socio-economic influences, gender roles and gender role expectations, balance of power, and socio-emotional climates based on the characters' action and dialogue.

(049J) Kelley, Samuel L. "The Evolution of Character Portrayals in the Films of Sidney Poitier, 1950-1978." Ph.D. dissertation, University of Michigan, 1980. (41/02A, p. 438)

In the 1950s and mid-1960s, Sidney Poitier emerged as the leading Black film actor. He became the first Black actor to win the academy award for Best Actor for his role in "Lilies of the Field" in 1964. After the late 1960s, however, Poitier's popularity as a mass hero began to wane because the assimilationist image which he projected was out-of-step with the Black nationalist mood which was sweeping the country. This study focuses on the emergence of Poitier as a major film star and his eventual decline in popularity in the late 1960s. An analysis is made of four of Poitier's major films: "No Way Out";

"Lillies of the Field"; "Guess Who's Coming to Dinner"; and "The Lost Man."

(050J) Marshall, Alexander C. "Representative Directors, Black Theatre Productions and Practices at Historically Black Colleges and Universities, 1968-1978." Ph.D. dissertation, Bowling Green State University, 1980.

An examination of the status of Black Theatre dramatic productions at historically Black colleges and universities with degree programs in Speech, Drama, Theatre and Communications is the subject addressed in this study. This researcher: (1) profiles the theatrical directors at these institutions focusing of their philosophies and practices; (2) describes and categorizes the Black plays produced between 1968 and 1978; (3) characterizes the practices in theatre management; and (4) discusses trends and some implications from the data collected.

(051J) Pounds, Michael C. "Details in Black: A Case Study Investigation and Analysis of the Content of the United States War Department Non-Fiction Motion Picture 'The Negro Soldier.'" (Volumes I and II). Ph.D. dissertation New York University, 1982.

The film, The Negro Soldier, was produced by the United States War Department in the interest of projecting a positive image of the Black American in World War II. Examining the social conditions surrounding the film's production and presenting a content analysis of The Negro Soldier, this study compares the film's portrayal of Black Americans with official government policy statements on the treatment of Black Americans in films. Pound makes the following assessment of The Negro Soldier. "Although some depictions were substantial improvements over Hollywood's Black stereotypes, others, in both civilian and military contexts, reflected negative racial attitudes."

(052J) Richard, Sandra L. "Sweet Meat from Le Roi: The Dramatic World of Amiri Baraka." Ph.D. dissertation, Stanford University, 1979.

In this study the researcher attempts to define the artistic sensibilities of Amiri Baraka (Le Roi Jones) through an analysis of this dramatist's plays. She also explores the relationship between Baraka's artistic sensibilities and the development of the Black aesthetic.

(053J) Washington, Rhonnie L. "The Relationship Between the White Critic and the Black Theatre, 1959-1969." Ph.D. dissertation, The University of Michigan, 1983.

The relationship between the Black theatre and the white critic is evaluated in this study. Reviews of plays by Black dramatists which were produced in New York between

1959 and 1969 and reviewed by three or more white critics are analyzed. One of the several conclusions drawn by Dr. Washington was: "The Black dramatist was patronized in an attempt to make the Black theatre, symbolically, an equal part of the American theatre."

(054J) Washington, Von Hugo. "An Evaluation of 'Purlie Victorious' and Its Impact on the American Theatrical Scene." Ph.D. dissertation, Wayne State University, 1979.

"Purlie Victorious" was one of the most successful musical comedies depicting the Black experience through the eyes of Black people ever produced on Broadway. The objective of this study is to describe the impact of "Purlie Victorious" on the American theatrical and social scene when it was first produced on Broadway in 1961. The reviews of "Purlie Victorious," which appeared in the press and the written critical commentaries by such noted theatrical historians as Loften Mitchell, Doris Abramson, and James V. Hatch, are analyzed by this researcher. A transcribed interview with Ossie Davis, the author of "Purlie Victorious," sheds light on the theories he employed in writing the musical comedy.

(055J) Williams, Mance R. "The Color of Black Theatre: A Critical Analysis of the Black Theatre Movement of the 1960s and 1970s." Ph.D. dissertation, University of Missouri-Columbia, 1980.

Although the plays of the Black Theatre Movement of the 1960s and 1970s successfully addressed the social, political and economic concerns of Black Americans, Black dramatists and performers despaired because of the absence of an effective critical approach to these plays as evidenced in reviews and other critical commentaries by theatrical critics. This study attempts to provide a historical and theoretical foundation for the critical evaluation of plays representative of the Black Theatre Movement by: (1) presenting a historical overview of the Black Theatre Movement from the 1920s through the 1970s; highlighting the influences of Amiri Baraka and Ed Bullins; (2) discussing the basic philosophical principles which guided the Movement; (3) analyzing the philosophical/social concepts found in the plays; and (4) describing other specific characteristics in the plays of the Black Theatre Movement.

(056J) Young, Artee F. "Lester Walton: Black Theatre 'Critic'." Ph.D. dissertation, The University of Michigan, 1980.

From 1908 to 1925, Lester Alger Walton--black critic, manager, journalist, and cultural and social historian, wrote a weekly theatrical column for the New York Age. In these critical commentaries, Walton laid the foundation for the criticism of Black drama. Young analyzes Walton's columns in an effort to evaluate his concepts of Black theatrical criticism.

K.
Critiquing Black Bards: Black Literary Criticism

BIBLIOGRAPHIC WORKS

(001K) Black American Writers: Bibliographic Essays. Edited by M. Thomas Inge, Maurice Duke, Jackson R. Bryer, New York: St. Martin's Press, 1978. 2v.

This two-volume work, according to its editors,

> "...is intended as an appraisal of the best biographical and critical writings about America's seminal black writers, as well as an identification of manuscript and special resources for continued study."

Volume I contains critical and biographical commentaries on early Black writers from the late eighteenth century through the Harlem Renaissance and Langston Hughes. Volume II includes critical works about Richard Wright, Ralph Ellison, James Baldwin and LeRoi Jones.

(002K) Campbell, Dorothy. Index to Black American Writers in Collective Biographies. Littleton, Colorado: Libraries Unlimited, 1983.

Biographical information appearing on approximately 1,900 Black American writers in 267 collective biographies is indexed in this unique work. The publication dates of the collective biographies indexed extend from 1837 to 1982. The following types of writers are included: creative writers, biographers, autobiographers, historians, pioneer journalists, literary critics, illustrators, scholar/bibliographers.

(003K) Fairbanks, Carol and Engeldinger, Eugene. Black American Fiction: A Bibliography. Metuchen, NJ: Scarecrow, 1978.

Limited only to works of fiction and criticism of fiction, this bibliography lists citations to books, short stories and articles by and about Black writers. Each entry contains: (1) name of author; (2) citations to short fiction; (3) citations to novels; (4) citations to biographical and critical writings about the author and his/her works; and (5) citations to book reviews.

(004K) Houston, Helen R. The Afro-American Novel, 1965-1975: A Descriptive Bibliography of Primary and Secondary Material. Troy, NY: Whitston, 1977.

The novels and critical commentaries on Black novelists who published between 1965 and 1975 are cited in this descriptive bibliography. Each entry contains the following information about the novelist: (1) a brief biographical statement; (2) a descriptive list of the novelist's works which were published from 1965 to 1975; and (3) a list of critical commentaries on the novelist's works.

(005K) Margolies, Edward; Bakish, David, eds. Afro-American Fiction, 1853-1976: A Guide to Information Sources. Detroit Gale, 1979 (American Literature, English Literature, and World Literature in English Information Guide Ser.: Vol. 25).

Focusing on works of fiction by Black writers which were published between 1853 and 1976, this comprehensive, but unannotated, bibliography is divided into four chapters. Chapter one is a checklist of novels. Short story collections by individual writers and anthologies of short stories by Black writers are cited in Chapter two. Citations to critical and biographical commentaries in books and periodicals on 15 major Black writers are presented in Chapter three. Chapter four is devoted to citations to bibliographies and general studies on Black fiction.

(006K) Rush, Theressa G.; Myers, Carol F.; Arata, Esther S. Black American Writers Past and Present: A Biographical and Bibliographical Dictionary. Metuchen, NJ: Scarecrow, 1975. 2v.

Containing information on more than 2,000 deceased and living Black American writers (and African and West Indian writers who live or publish in the United States), this reference work is one of the most comprehensive bio-bibliographies on Black writers to appear to date. Arranged alphabetically by author, each entry includes: (1) name of author; (2) birthdate and place; (3) deathdate; (4) education; (5) career highlights; (6) bibliography of published works; (7) bibliography of biographical sources and literary criticism on the author's work. An excellent bibliography of books and journal articles on Black writing appears at the end of volume II.

(007K) Turner, Darwin T. Afro-American Writers. New York: Appleton-Century-Crofts, Educational Division, 1970.

Aimed at graduate and advanced undergraduate students in Afro-American literature, this unannotated bibliography focuses on works published during the twentieth century. Although it includes sections with citations to general and related works on Afro-American literary history and criticism, its major emphasis is on citations to works by individual Afro-American authors and critical commentaries on their works.

COLLECTIVE BIOGRAPHICAL WORKS

(008K) Bailey, Leaonead P., comp. Broadside Authors and Artists: An Illustrated Biographical Directory. Detroit: Broadside Press, 1974.

In the 1960s and 1970s, Dudley Randall's Broadside Press in Detroit published the works of a host of young, aspiring and seasoned Black writers. Biographical information on 192 Black authors, and a few white authors, who published with Broadside Press and the Heritage Press Series, which was edited by Paul Bremen in England and distributed by Braodside Press, are included in this directory.

(009K) Page, James A. comp. Selected Black American Authors: An Illustrated Bio-bibliography. Boston: G. K. Hall, 1977.

Biographical sketches of 450 Black authors, whose works were published from the Colonial Period to the late 1970s, appear in this compilation. A few Black publishers of newspapers and journals have also been included. However, Black authors who have published their own works have been excluded. Entries for 285 biographies contain the author's photograph. Arranged alphabetically by author, entries list the following information: (1) name of author; (2) birth/death date; (3) education; (4) mailing address; (5) career highlights; (6) published works; (7) honors and awards; (8) sidelights; and (9) references to information on the author.

(010K) Shockley, Ann A.; Chandler, Sue P. Living Black American Authors: A Biographical Directory. New York: Bowker, 1973.

The first biographical dictionary on Black authors, this reference work was compiled primarily with author questionnaires. It contains biographical information on Black authors who were living in 1977. Black authors included: (1) have written books; (2) have works in progress; (3) have published journals on periodicals. Completed entries contain: (1) name and occupation; (2) place and date of birth; (3) education; (4) family; (5) professional experience; (6) memberships; (7) awards; (8) publications; (9) mailing address.

(011K) Tate, Claudia, ed. Black Women Writers at Work. New York: Continuun, 1983.

Fourteen Black women writers are interviewed in this collection. "The interviews," the editor observes, "are fashioned so that the writers share their conscious motives for selecting particular characters, situations, and techniques to depict their ideas. The fourteen writers are Maya Angelou, Toni Cade Bambara, Alexis Deveaux, Nikki Giovanni, Kristen Hunter, Gayl Jones, Audre Lorde, Toni Morrison, Sonia Sanchez, Alice Walker, Margaret Walker, and Sherley Anne Williams.

HANDBOOKS AND INDEXES

(012K) Chapman, Dorothy H. Index to Black Poetry. Boston: G. K. Hall, 1974.

A total of 94 books and pamphlets of individual Black poets and 33 anthologies containing Black poetry are indexed in this reference work. Poems are accessed by three indexes: a title and first line index; an author index and a subject index.

(013K) Index to Black American Literary Anthologies. Compiled under the direction of Jessamine S. Kallenbach. Sponsored by the Center for Educational Resources, Eastern Michigan University, Ypsilanti, Michigan. Boston: G. K. Hall, 1979.

Over 140 anthologies containing the publications of Black authors in all literary genres are indexed in this reference work. Section I, which includes the main entries, is arranged by author. Each entry cites: (1) name of author; (2) genre or genres in which the author writes; (3) titles of writings with references to the anthology. Section II is a title index with reference to Section I.

(014K) Southgate, Robert L. Black Plots and Black Characters: A Handbook for Afro-American Literature. Syracuse, NY: Gaylord Professional Publications, 1971.

Divided into five sections, this ready reference source is a compendium of useful information on Afro-American literature. Part I, "Plot Summaries," presents summaries and short commentaries on novels, speeches and poems by Afro-Americans between the late 18th century and the mid-1970s. Part II, "A Short Companion for Afro-American Literature and History," is a glossary of terms, biographies, and concepts in Afro-American history and literature. Part III, "Author-Bibliography," lists citations to works by and about individual Afro-American writers. Part IV, "General Bibliography," is a classified list of works on various subjects in Afro-American history and literature.

In the "Chronological Index," important dates in Afro-American history and literature are cited chronologically.

CRITICAL LITERARY COMMENTARIES, ESSAYS AND TREATISES

(015K) Baker, Houston A., Jr. Blues, Idealogy and Afro-American Literature: A Vernacular Theory. Chicago: University of Chicago Press, 1984.

The blues, as Baker observes in this work, is an integral part of Afro-American cultural expression. The objective of this study he states in the following terms.

> "In my study as a whole, I attempt persuasively to demonstrate that a blues matrix (as a vernacular trope for American cultural explanation in general) possesses enormous force for the study of literature, criticism and culture."

(016K) Baker, Houston A., Jr. The Journey Back: Issues in Black Literature and Criticism. Chicago: University of Chicago Press, 1980.

Baker attempts to develop a new investigative strategy to apply to Black literature. The framework which he suggests is named the "Anthropology of Art." It is an inter-disciplinary approach utilizing concepts advanced by symbolic Anthropologist, Clifford Geertz, Anthropologist Edmund Leech, and Afro-American poet/literary critic, Larry Neal.

(017K) Barthald, Bonnie J. Black Time: Fiction of Africa, the Caribbean and the United States. New Haven: Yale University Press, 1981.

The novelist, unlike the playwrights has the freedom to manipulate time in his genre. Focusing on the use of time in Black fiction, Barthold discusses: (1) the historical background of Black fiction and the use of time by Black writers; (2) certain characteristics, themes and forms in Black fiction related to the use of time; and (3) representative novels of Black writers which illustrate the use of time in relation to the Black experience.

(018K) Black American Prose Theory. Edited by Joe Weixlmann and Chester Fontenat. Greenwood, FL: Penkville Publishing Co., 1984. (Studies in Black American Literature, vol. 1).

This new literary annual is devoted to scholarly investigations focusing on the theoretical aspects of Black American literature. This volume explores the theory of

Black prose. Among the eight essays are: "Visionaries, Mystics, and Revolutionaries: Narrative Posturis in Black Fiction," by Chester J. Fontenot; "The South as Woman: Chimeric Images of Emasculation in Just Above My Head, by Trudier Harris; and "The Blackness of Blackness": A Critique of the Sign and the Signifying Monkey," by Henry Louis Gates, Jr.

(019K) Black Literature and Literary Theory, edited by Henry Louis Gates, Jr. New York: Metuchen, 1984.

Many Black writers and critics have argued that white critics trained in the western literary tradition cannot realistically evaluate Black literary text. They assert that the relationship between Black texts and western literary tradition is problematic. In this collection of essays, thirteen critics discuss how applicable western literary tradition is to the reading of Black texts produced in the African, Caribbean or Afro-American literary traditions. The thirteen contributors are: Sunday O. Anozie; Anthony Appiah; Houston A. Baker, Jr.; Kimberly W. Benston; Jay Edwards; Henry Louis Gates, Jr.; Barbara Johnson; James A. Snead; Wale Soyinka; Robert B. Stepto; Mary Helen Washington; and Susan Wills.

(020K) Black Women Writers (1950-1980): A Critical Evaluation. Edited by Mari Evans. With an introduction by Stephen Henderson. New York: Anchor Press/Doubleday, 1984.

Fifteen contemporary Black American women writers and poets are presented and analyzed in this unique collection. Excerpts from the writings and critical commentaries on the works of the following Black women writers and poets are included: Maya Angelou; Toni Cade Bambara; Gwendolyn Brooks; Alice Childress; Lucille Clifton; Mari Evans; Nikki Giovanni; Audre Lorde; Paule Marshall; Toni Morrison; Carolyn Rodgers; Sonia Sanchez; Alice Walker; and Margaret Walker.

(021K) Bone, Robert A. Down Home: A History of Afro-American Short Fiction from Its Beginnings to the End of the Harlem Renaissance. New York: G. P. Putnam's Sons, 1975.

Pointing to the Black American's historical attachment to the Protestant tradition with emphasis on the Bible and the Black American's attraction to the natural beauty of his southern homeland, Bone advances, in this work, the thesis that the pastoral mode dominated the short fiction of Black American writers between 1885 and the mid-1930s. To illustrate this thesis, Bone critically analyzes early Afro-American folktales and the short fiction of Paul L. Dunbar, Charles Chesnutt, Zora Hurston, Rudolph Fisher, Claude McKay, Eric Walrond, Jean Toomer, Langston Hughes and Arna Bontemps.

(022K) Bone, Robert A. The Negro Novel in America. Rev. ed.

New Haven: Yale University Press, 1965.

Over 100 novels by Black Americans published between 1890 and 1963 are surveyed in this classic critical study of the Black American novel. Unlike previous studies of the Black American novel, which have treated it as a social document, Bone critically evaluates the Black novel in this study as a work of art.

> "I have tried to avoid the Parrington fallacy by placing strong emphasis upon form--attempting to establish the work of art in its own right before viewing it as part of the cultural process."

(023K) Bruck, Peter; Karrer, Wolfgang, ed. The Afro-American Novel Since 1960. Philadelphia: John Benjamins North America, Inc., 1982.

The social history of the Black novel from 1960 to 1980 is reconstructed in this collection of critical essays by white American and European critics. The 11 Black novels discussed are: Brown Girl, Brownstones, by Paule Marshall; Night Song, by John A. Williams; A Different Drummer, by William Melvin Kelley; The Catacombs by William Demby; The Wig, by Charles Wright; Yellow-Black Radio Broke Down, by Ishmael Reed; The Third Life of Grange Copeland, by Alice Walker; The Autobiography of Miss Jane Pittman, by Ernest Gaines; Train Whitle Guitar, by Albert Murray; Who Is Angelina, by Al Young; and Song of Solomon, by Toni Morrison. A chronological checklist of Afro-American novels published from 1945 through 1980 is included.

(024K) Bruck, Peter, ed. The Black American Short Story in the Twentieth Century. Philadelphia: Benjamins North America, 1977.

This collection contains critical essays on the Black short story. These essays were written between 1889 (Charles Waddell Chesnutt's "Sheriff's Children," by Hartmat K. Selker) and 1965 (Amiri Baraka's "The Alternative," by John Wakefield). The essayists attempt to provide new points of orientation for the critical analyses of the Black short story.

(025K) Christian, Barbara Black Women Novelists: The Development of a Tradition, 1892-1976. Westport, CT: Greenwood Press, 1980.

The literary tradition of the Black woman novelist is analyzed in this work as well as the image of the Black woman in literature. Covering the years from 1860 through 1960, Christian critically reivews the work of Black women novelists and the image of the Black woman projected in the literature of the period. The craft, ideas and creative artistry of three contemporary Black women novelists are discussed substantively in the study: Paule Marshall, Toni Morrison and Alice Walker.

(026K) Davis, Arthur P. From the Dark Tower: Afro-American Writers (1900-1960). Washington, D.C.: Howard University Press, 1974.

Davis presents a critical survey of significant Black American writers from 1900 through 1960 in this volume. This handbook of essays is a classic contribution to Afro-American literary criticism.

(027K) Davis, Charles T. Black is the Color of the Cosmos: Essays on Afro-American Literature, 1942-1981. Edited by Henry Louis Gates, Jr. Foreword by A. Bartlett Giamatti. New York: Garland Publishing Co., 1982.

The late Charles T. Davis (1918-1981), formerly Professor of English and Chairman of Afro-American Studies at Yale, was a leading Black literary critic who wrote and lectured widely on Walt Whitman, E. A. Robinson, Lucy Larcom, as well as such Black writers as Richard Wright, Robert Hayden and Ralph Ellison. In this collection of essays, written between 1942 and 1981 and published posthumously, Davis defines the complex nature of the Afro-American literary tradition. The essays are grouped under three headings: "Theories of Black Literature and Culture"; "The Structure of the Afro-American Literary Tradition"; and "On Wright, Ellison and Baldwin." A bibliography of Charles T. Davis' writings is included in an appendix.

(028K) Gayle, Addison, Jr. The Way of the New World: The Black Novel in America. Garden City, NY: Anchor Press/Doubleday, 1975.

The changing world vision of Black novelists and writers from 1853 through the early 1970s is analyzed in this highly interpretative study. Gayle observes.

> "...at long last, form and structure were recognized as little more than cousins to content, and the Black novelist, machine gunner in the cause of mankind, prepared to move forward in the most monumental undertaking of the twentieth century."

(029K) Gloster, Hugh M. Negro Voices in American Fiction. Chaptel Hill: The University of North Carolina Press, 1948. (Reprinted, New York: Russell and Russell, 1965).

Surveying the fiction published by Black writers from Charles W. Chesnutt to Richard Wright, this study, one of the earliest of its kind, discusses the themes and attitudes embodied in the Black fiction of the period. The work, as Gloster relates, is not a literary study:

> "...this book is concerned not so much with literary appraisal as with racial expression."

Nonetheless, it is a valuable source for documenting the literary efforts of some well-known and many lesser-known Black writers who published in the first half of the twentieth century.

(030K) Harris, Trudier. From Mammies to Militants: Domestics in Black American Literature. Philadelphia: Temple University Press, 1982.

Black domestics who are prominent characters in the literary works of eleven Black writers from Charles W. Chesnutt's The Marrow of Tradition (1901) to Ed Bullens' The Gentlemen Caller (1969) are discussed in this work. This interdisciplinary study utilizes analytical techniques from folklore, sociology, history, psychology, and literary criticism in the examination of Black domestics created by the eleven writers.

(031K) Hughes, Carl M. The Negro Novelist: A Discussion of the Writings of American Negro Novelists, 1940-1950. New York: The Citadel Press, 1953.

The 1940s was an extremely productive decade for Black American novelists, according to Hughes, and critical reception was favorable.

> "In retrospect the forties proved to be a productive period for the Negro novelist. Actually critical reception favored an increasingly large number of novels because of their high literary merit. This book, through critical analysis, develops the thesis that Negro novelists of the forties broadened their perspective."

In this critical survey of Black American novels published in the 1940s, Hughes discusses the works of Richard Wright, Zora Neale Hurston, Frank Yerby, Chester Himes, Ann Petry, J. Saundera Redding and several others.

(032K) Skonne, Chidi. From DuBois to Van Vechten: The Early New Negro Literature. Westport, CT: Greenwood Press, 1981.

Many Black writers during the Harlem Renaissance were inspired by W.E.B. DuBois' Souls of Black Folk which was published in 1903. Most of these writers, also, acknowledge the influence of Carl Van Vetchen's novel Nigger Heaven (1926) on their writings. Skonne, in this study, discusses the nature of the influence of these two works on the Harlem Renaissance writers.

(033K) Loggins, Vernon. The Negro Author: His Development in America to 1900. New York: Columbia University Press, 1931. (Reprinted: Port Washington, NY: Kennikat Press, Inc., 1964).

Surveying the fiction and non-fiction writings published by Black Americans from 1760 to 1900, this work was the first comprehensive scholarly study to appear on Black American authorship. Loggins, however, found little artistic value in the Black literature of the period.

> "Although productive of little that is truly artistic, that field extends far and wide."

In spite of Loggins' negative assessment, this study documents publications of major and minor Black writers before 1900, and it contains an extensive bibliography of the publications of Black Americans before 1900.

(034K) Lee, A. Robert, ed. Black Fiction: New Studies in the Afro-American Novel Since 1945. New York: Barnes and Noble, 1980.

The eleven essays in this collection, by American and British critics, discuss the changing artistic developments in the Afro-American novel from Richard Wright's Native Son (1940) to Leon Forrest's The Bloodworth Orphans (1977). Entire essays are devoted to the works of Richard Wright, Langston Hughes, Ann Petry, Ralph Ellison, James Baldwin, LeRoi Jones, and Ishmael Reed.

(035K) Payne, Ladell. Black Novelists and the Southern Literary Tradition. Athens: The University of Georgia Press, 1981.

Several prominent Black novelists lived in the South during their formative years. Their works, like those of southern white novelists, reflect southern values. In this seminal study, Ladell Payne explores the relationships of five Black southern-born novelists - Charles Waddell Chesnutt, James Weldon Johnson, Jean Toomer, Richard Wright, and Ralph Ellison - to white southern novelists.

(036K) Scruggs, Charles. The Sage of Harlem: H. L. Menchin and the Black Writers of the 1920s. Baltimore: Johns Hopkins University Press, 1984.

As the editor of The American Mercury, 1925-33, H. L. Menchin, who had been called "The Literary Dictator of America," in the 1920s, published several Harlem Renaissance writers. During his tenure as editor of The American Mercury, thirty-four articles by Black writers appeared in the journal by such writers as James Weldon Johnson, W.E.B. DuBois, and J. A. Rogers. In this enlightening study, Charles Scruggs explores Menchen's influence on the Black writers of the Harlem Renaissance.

(037K) Sekora, John; Turner, Darwin T., eds. The Art of the Slave Narrative: Original Essays in Criticism and Theory. Macomb, IL: Western Illinois University, 1982.

Eleven essays in this collection critically evaluate the slave narrative. These essays discuss the following characteristics of the slave narrative: origins of the genre; its terminal dates; its nature and influence; and its main conventions, structural elements, and rhetorical strategies.

(038K) Wade-Gayles, Gloria. No Crystal Stair: Visions of Race and Sex in Black Women's Fiction. New York: The Pilgrim Press, 1984.

Using selected novels written by Black women between 1946 and 1976, this study attempts to explain the images of Black women projected in these works.

(039K) Whitlow, Roger. Black American Literature. Totowa, NJ: Littlefield, Adams and Co., 1974.

The history and development of Black American literature is critically discussed in this general survey which covers the years from 1746 to the early 1970s. A splendid 1,520-title unannotated bibliography adds to the reference value of this comprehensive work.

CRITICAL COMMENTARIES ON THE LIVES AND WORKS OF SELECTED BLACK AMERICAN WRITERS

(040K) Barksdale, Richard K. Langston Hughes: The Poet and His Critics. Chicago: American Library Association, 1977.

In this chronological assessment of the poetry of Langston Hughes, Barksdale evaluates the critical commentaries which have appeared on Hughes poetic works from 1926 through the late 1970s. An extensive, bibliography of Hughes' publications and the critical works on his poetry is included.

(041K) Fabre, Michel. The Unfinished Quest of Richard Wright. Translated from the French by Isabel Barzun. New York: Morrow, 1973.

This monumental treatise is the most comprehensive study to appear on Richard Wright to date. Researching for more than 12 years, Fabre examined Wright's personal papers, interviewed hundreds of personal friends from

Wright's childhood and adult years, and critically evaluated Wright's published and unpublished works. The result of Fabre's efforts is a meticulous assessment of Richard Wright's life, artistry, and humanism by a brilliant literary critic of American literature.

(042K) Flasch, Jay. Melvin B. Tolson. New York: Twayne, 1972.

Although Melvin B. Tolson has received relatively little critical attention, three books of poems by B. Tolson have been highly acclaimed by major critics. They are Rendezvous with America (1944), Libretto for the Republic of Liberia (1953), and Harlem Gallery: Book I, The Curator (1965). In this critical survey of Tolson's works, Flasch examines his published and unpublished poetry, prose and drama.

(043K) Hatcher, John. From the Auroral Darkness: The Life and Poetry of Robert Hayden. Oxford, England: Ronald, 1984.

After presenting a brief synopsis of the life of the late "Poet Laureate," Robert Hayden, John Hatcher critically examines his poetry. Hayden's ten volumes of poetry is treated chronologically by Hatcher to insure the "continuity of his art." Since many of the early volumes of Hayden's poetry are out of print, the table of contents of all ten volumes are included in the appendix as an aid to the reader.

(044K) Hemenway, Robert E. Zora Neale Hurston: A Literary Biography. With a foreward by Alice Walker. Urbana: University of Illinois Press, 1977.

Writer, folklorist and scholar, Zora Neale Hurston was one of the most colorful and prolific Black women writers of the first half of the twentieth century. Robert Hemenway's perceptive biography brilliantly recaptures Hurston's life, focusing on her literary activities as well as critically examining her works and the response of the public to them.

(045K) Martin, Jay Martin, ed. A Singer in the Dawn: Reinterpretations of Paul Laurence Dunbar. New York: Dodd, Mead, 1975.

The fourteen essays included in this volume were presented as papers at the Centenary Conference on Paul Laurence Dunbar held at the University of California-Irvine in 1972. The poetry, prose and life of Paul Laurence Dunbar are examined from new perspectives. Among some of the contributions were: "The Relevance of Paul Laurence Dunbar," by Arna Bontemps; "Paul Laurence Dunbar: The Poet and the Myths," by Darwin Turner; "Literature as Catharsis: The Novels of Paul Laurence Dunbar," by Addison Gayle, Jr.

(046K) Millikin, Stephen. Chester Hemis: A Critical Appraisal. Columbia: University of Missouri Press, 1976.

The novels, novellas and short stories of Chester Himes are critically evaluated in this study. In his assessment of Himes' work, Millikin alludes to episodes in Himes' craftsmanship, and his use of recurring themes.

(047K) O'Daniel, Therman B., ed. James Baldwin: A Critical Evaluation. Washington, D.C.: Howard University Press, 1977.

Twenty-three critical essays, written by members of the College Language Association, examine the novels, essays short stories, plays, dialogues and scenarios of James Baldwin. An extensive classified work by and about James Baldwin is included.

(048K) O'Daniel, Therman B., ed. Jean Toomer: A Critical Evaluation. Washington, D.C.: Howard University Press, 1983.

With more than 40 essays by 39 contributors, this collection presents an indepth and broad treatment of Jean Toomer. This volume represents the most recent critical analysis of Toomer's works.

(049K) O'Meally, Robert G. The Craft of Ralph Ellison. Cambridge: Harvard University Press, 1980.

The works of Ralph Ellison published between 1937 and 1979 are critically examined in the study. O'Meally, focusing on the characters and the fictional world in which they exist, identifies certain themes which recur in Ellison's works and discusses his use of folklore.

(50K) Shaw, Harry B. Gwendolyn Brooks. Boston: Twayne Publishers, 1980.

In this study Gwendolyn Brooks' poetry is analyzed in terms of its social themes. These themes are death, the fall from glory, the laybrinth and survival.

(051K) Sollors, Werner. Amiri Baraka/Le Roi Jones: The Quest for a "Populist Modernism." New York: Columbia University Press, 1978.

In this study Sollors presents an interpretative survey of Baraka's writings. After discussing briefly significant facts about Baraka's life in an introduction, Sollors describes his artistic socialization in New York's Bohemian community of the 1950s. A critical analysis of Baraka's works as well as his political developments are discussed.

SELECTED PERIODICAL ARTICLES

(052K) Benston, Kimberly W. "I 'Yam What I Am: Naming and Unnaming in Afro-American Literature." Black American Literature Forum. (Spring 1982):3-11.

After the Civil War many ex-slaves established a new identity by re-naming themselves. More recently new members of the Black Muslims replaced their "slave" surnames with the Mysterious "X." Kimberly Benston explores the psychological ramifications of the re-naming process as revealed in the works on several Black writers, focusing on the works of Ralph Ellison and Jay Wright.

(053K) Brown, Michael R. "Homage to Robert Hayden, 1913-1980." Commentary. 70(September 1980):66-9.

Robert Hayden was one of the leading American poets of his generation. In this enlightening memoir, Michael Brown recollects significant encounters with Hayden during their friendship.

(054K) Clarke, Graham. "Beyond Realism: Recent Black Fiction and the Language of the Real Thing." Black American Literature Forum. 16(Spring 1982):43-8.

Clarke observes that the vocabulary of some contemporary Black realist novelists go beyond the limits of realism to describe the ruthlessness inherent in the Black experience. The language of these writers seek to create "the reality of the word itself." The works of novelist Julian Mayfield, Ronald L. Fair, Robert Deane Pharr and Hal Bennett are discussed to illustrate this new development in the use of language by Black writers.

(055K) Gates, Henry Louis, Jr. "Blackness of Blackness: A Critique of the Sign and the Signifying Monkey." Critical Inquiry. 9(June 1983):685-723.

"Signifying" in the Black community is the narrative language of the trickster which is used to achieve a variety of ends. In this article, Gates, realizing its potential for literary critical theory, explains "signifying" as an Afro-American narrative parody. He employs it in a reading of Ishmael Reed's novel, Mumbo Jumbo, as a "signifying" literary composition of the Afro-American narrative tradition.

(056K) Hansell, William H. "Three Artists in Melvin B. Tolson's Harlem Gallery." Black American Literature Forum. 18 (Fall 1984):122-127.

The first and final chapters of poet Melvin B. Tolson's

classic poem Harlem Gallery introduces and reviews the aesthetic principles used throughout the poem. Hansell summarizes these chapters and discusses their characters in the poem who are embodiments of the aesthetic principles: John Laugart, Hideho Heights and Mister Starks.

(057K) Hedin, Raymond. "The Structure of Emotion in Black American Fiction." Novel: A Forum on Fiction. 16(Fall 1982):35-54.

Anger against whites in the slave narrative, which was directed towards a white audience, was muted and structured by the narrator in an effort to prove to the reader that the narrator was a human being unworthy of enslavement. Hedin asserts the structuring of anger against whites by Afro-American writers is characteristic of the Afro-American literary tradition and is evident in the works of several Black novelists today. The techniques of internal organization utilized by some contemporary Black novelists in their works to express anger towards whites are examined by Hedin in this essay.

(058K) Pinsker, Sanford. "A conversation with Etheridge Knight." Black American Literature Forum. 18(Spring 1984):11-14.

Poet Etheridge Knight, since the publication of his first book, Poems From Prison, in 1968, has become one of the more popular Black poets. In this interview, conducted on April 6, 1983, at Franklin and Marshall College, Knight talks about: (1) the status of Black poetry in American letters in the 1980s as opposed to the 1960s and 1970s; (2) Black aesthetics; and (3) the duty of the poet.

(059K) Rampersad, Arnold. "Universal and the Particular in Afro-American Poetry." CLA Journal. 25(September 1981):1-17.

White literary critics have frequently asserted that Black literature does not embody universal concepts. Rampersad refutes this assessment by discussing universal concepts in the works and pronouncements of several Black writers and critics from the early twentieth century to the late 1970s.

(060K) Sheffey, R. T. "Rhetorical Structure in Contemporary Afro-American Poetry." CLA Journal. 24(Spring 1980): 97-107.

Most of the critical commentary on the new Black poetry, Sheffrey observes, focuses on the themes inherent in this poetry as a critical category. In this essay, Sheffrey examines the syntatic foundations of respresentative Black poems in an effort to show how the poetic process and aesthetic are enriched.

(061K) Ward, Jerry W., Jr. "A Black and Crucial Enterprise:

An Interview with Houston A. Baker, Jr." Black American Literature Forum. 16(Summer 1982:51-8.

In this interview, conducted at Tougaloo College on February 20, 1980, literary critic, Houston A. Baker, Jr., substantively discusses some critical issues related to Afro-American literature. Among some of the topics addressed are: the relations of Black critics with Black readers; the impact of the Civil Rights movement on Black writers; white critics on Black literature.

SELECTED DISSERTATIONS

(062K) Burnette, R. V. "Charles Waddell Chestnutt: The Published Fiction." Ph.D. dissertation, Rutgers University, the State University of New Jersey, (New Brunswick), 1984.

Focusing on the sociological aspects, this study examines the published fiction of Charles Waddell Chesnutt. In his analysis, Burnette emphasizes how Chesnutt in his fiction responded to the hostile racial ideologies which were prevalent during the last decade of the nineteenth century and the early decades of the twentieth century.

(063K) Chambers, Kenneth L. "In Pursuit of the Dream: An Analysis and Evaluation of the Writings of John A. Williams." Ph.D. dissertation, The University of Iowa, 1983.

Chambers conducts a thematic analysis of John A. Williams' fictional works that were published between 1960 and 1980. The four recurring themes identified were: Black writer/professional as victim; the Black community as victim; the interracial marriage; and a sympathetic portrayal of Black life and culture. These themes, Chambers concludes, were altered by changes in Williams' idealogical stance during his career.

(064K) Clark, Norris B. "The Black Aesthetic Reviewed: A Critical Examination of the writings of Imamu Amiri Baraka, Gwendolyn Brooks, and Toni Morrison." Ph.D. dissertation, Cornell University, 1980.

After reviewing several opinions on Black aesthetics advanced by Black intellectuals, Clark discusses the absurdities to which an advocacy of Black aesthetics can lead. The early egocentric poetry and the late ethnocentric poetry of Imamu Amiri Baraka and Gwendolyn Brooks as well as the works of Toni Morrison are analyzed. Clark concludes that the late ethnocentric poetry Baraka and Brooks fail to meet Black aesthetics criteria.

(065K) Davis, Jane M. "The Peculiar Kind of Hell: The Role

of Power in the Novels of Richard Wright." Ph.D. dissertation, Stanford University, 1984.

Five of Richard Wright's novels are analyzed in this study to determine the role of power in his works. The novels are: Native Son; The Outsider; The Long Dream; Lawd Today; and The Savage Holiday. Davis' analysis focuses on four topics: (1) the impact of various sources of power on Wright's personal life; (2) Wright's fictional portrayal of fear of power; (3) Wright's depiction of women as a source of power; (4) Wright's portrayal of the devastating effects of power on people who are without power.

(066K) Davis, Mary K. "The Historical Slave Revolt and the Literary Imagination (Douglass, Melville, Bontemps, Styron). Ph.D. dissertation, The University of North Carolina at Chapel Hill, 1984.

The portrayal of the slave revolt in five fictional works is explored in this study. The works are: The Heroic Slave, by Frederick Douglass (1953), which treats the mutiny aboard the American ship, "Creole," in 1841; Benito Creno, by Herman Melville (1855), based on the mutiny on the Spanish slave ship, "Tryal," in 1804; Black Thunder, by Arna Bontemps (1936), which deals with the Gabriel Prosser conspiracy of 1800; Drums at Dusk, by Arna Bontemps (1939), which centers on the opening phases of the Haitian Revolution between 1791 and 1804; and William Styron's The Confessions of Nat Turner (1967), which focuses on the Nat Turner Revolt on 1831.

(067K) Gilchrist, Loretta. "The Prison Literature of Chester B. Himes," Ph.D. dissertation, Bowling Green State University, 1983.

The prison writings of Chester Himes, while he was incarcerated in the Ohio State Penitentiary in the 1930s, have been neglected by critics. Gilchrist analyzes the short stories and a novel, Cast the First Stone, which Himes wrote in prison and attempts to show how various elements in these writings are further developed in later works by Himes.

(068K) Gissendanner, John M. "The 'Nether' Channel: A Study of Faulkner's Black Characters." Ph.D. dissertation, University of California, San Diego, 1982.

Despite his southern literary heritage, William Faulkner, Gissendanner claims, attempted to render Black American characters in his novels with dignity. In this study, Gissendanner examines Black characterization in Faulkner's novels.

(069K) Henderson, Mae G. "In Another Country: Afro-American Expatriate Novelists in France, 1946-1974 (Black Exile Literature). Ph.D. dissertation, Yale University, 1983.

The lives and selected works of four Black American novelists living in France between 1946 and 1974 are examined in this study. The novelists and their selected novels are: Richard Wright (The Outsider); Chester Himes (A Case of Rape); James Baldwin (Giovanni's Room); and William Gardner Smith (The Stone Face).

(070K) Hogue, Willie L. "To Saddle Time: Sociocriticism and the Afro-American Text." Ph.D. dissertation, Stanford University, 1980.

Arguing that the traditional English and American literary theories of realism and reflectionism are inadequate for evaluating Afro-American literary texts, Hogue develops a new model entitled "Sociocriticism." He claims that "sociocriticism" is:

> "...capable of discerning the various ways in which modes of social production are articulated with literary production."

Using "Sociocriticism," Hogue investigates Alice Walker's The Third Life of Grange Copeland and Ernest J. Gaines' The Autobiography of Miss Jane Pittman.

(071K) Holt, Elvin. "Zora Neale Hurston and the Politics of Race: A Study in Selected Nonfictional Works." Ph.D. dissertation, University of Kentucky, 1983.

The racial politics of Zora Neale Hurston were decidedly conservative. She was intensely patriotic, opposed to social protest, and believed that Blacks should use their ingenuity to rise above racism. In this study, the non-fiction prose works, including Tell My Horse and Dust Tracks Upon A Road, are analyzed to document Hurston's attitudes on race politics.

(072K) Hughes, Joanne C. "Elements of the Confessional Mode in the Novels of James Baldwin: 1954-1979." Ph.D. dissertation, Northern Illinois University, 1980.

The confessional mode in six novels by James Baldwin are analyzed in this study. Hughes' analysis is based on the confessional mode as defined and discussed in Peter M. Axthelm's The Modern Confessional Novel. Hughes concludes:

> "Thus, Baldwin has more artistic and formal success with a limited narrative situation and thematic concern, as in Go Tell It on the Moutain, Giovanni's Room, and If Beale Street Could Talk, than with the more complex narrative situations and multiple thematic concerns that he posits in Another Country, Tell Me How Long the Train's Been Gone, and Just Above My Head."

(073K) McCauley, Mary S. "Alex Haley, A Southern Griot: A Literary Biography (Tennessee)." Ph.D. dissertation, George Peabody College for Teachers of Vanderbilt University, 1983.

Presenting the pertinent facts of Haley's life, this biography attempts to show how his life finds expression in his writings. Haleys' early life in Henning, Tennessee, the years in the United States Coast Guard, and the early successes as a writer are discussed in this study.

(074K) McIver, Dorothy J. "Stepchild in Harlem: The Literary Career of Wallace Thurman (New York)." Ph.D. dissertation, The University of Alabama, 1983.

Arriving in Harlem in 1925 at the height of the Harlem Renaissance, Wallace Thurman quickly became one of the leaders of this movement. Thurman distinguished himself as a novelist, playwright, editor, and literary critic. McIver examines Wallace Thurman's life, career and literary works and attempts to assess his place in American literary history.

(075K) Nwankruo, N'kem. "Cultural Primitivism and Related Ideas in Jean Toomer's 'Cane'." Ph.D. dissertation, Indiana University, 1982.

Utilizing the documentary history and related ideas set forth by Arthur Lovejoy and George Boas on primitivism, Kwankruo developed categories in which he designed a framework for the critical evaluation of Jean Toomer's _Cane_. Lovejoy and Boas' typologies were used to develop thematic paradigms for this analysis. Nwankruo concludes that the creation of _Cane_ by Toomer was a response to the author's discontent with civilization and his idealization of the primitive.

(076K) Pettis, Joyce Owens. "The Search for a Usable Past: A Study of Black Historical Fiction." Ph.D. dissertation, The University of North Carolina at Chapel Hill, 1983.

Relatively little historical fiction has been produced by Black writers. During the 1930s and the 1960s, however, Black writers did publish novels based on Afro-American history. In this study Pettis analyzes and discusses these works of historical fiction.

(077K) Smith, Valerie A. "'The Singer of One's Soul': Storytelling in the Fiction of James Weldon Johnson, Richard Wright, Ralph Ellison and Toni Morrison." Ph.D. dissertation, University of Virginia, 1982.

The ability of the protagonist to understand and articulate his/her life in four novels by Black writers is the subject of this study. The four novels are James Weldon Johnson's _Autobiography of the Ex-_

Colored Man; Richard Wright's Native Son; Ralph Ellison's Invisible Man; and Toni Morrison's Song of Solomon.

L. With a Sense of Pride: Black Cultural and Intellectual History

BIBLIOGRAPHICAL WORKS

(001L) Perry, Margaret. The Harlem Renaissance: An Annotated Bibliography and Commentary. New York: Garland Publishing Company, 1982.

Containing over 700 annotated citations on the Harlem Renaissance, this splendid work is a comprehensive bibliography of published and unpublished sources on the period. It lists citations to: (1) bibliographical and reference material; (2) literary histories; (3) general studies and studies of several authors; (4) studies of individual authors, miscellaneous articles; (5) anthologies; (6) library and other special collections; and (7) dissertations and thesis. No works are included which were published after 1980. Margaret Perry's commentary on the Harlem Renaissance provides an excellent introduction to the study of the period.

DICTIONARIES

(002L) The Harlem Renaissance: A Historical Dictionary for the Era. Edited by Bruce Kellner. Westport, CT: Greenwood Press, 1984.

The years of the Harlem Renaissance, delineated by Kellner from 1917 to 1935, are covered in this encyclopedic work. Entries from 50 to 1,500 words are included for significant personalities, events, locales and artistic works associated with the period. Among the entries for artistic works are plots of novels, dramas, and musical entertainments. Biographical entries are presented for major and minor personalities who were active in the Harlem Renaissance. Five important appendixes follow the main body of the work. They are: Appendix A, a chronology of key events during the Harlem Renaissance; Appendix B, chronological listing of books by and about Black Americans published during the period; Appendix C, a list of plays and musical entertainments by and about Black Americans produced between 1917 and 1935; Appendix D, a list of serial publications and newspapers with articles on the Harlem Renaissance; and Appendix E, a glossary of slang used during the period.

PUBLISHED CORRESPONDENCE

(003L) Bontemps, Arna W. Arna Bontemps - Langston Hughes Letters, 1925-1967. Selected and edited by Charles H. Nichols. New York: Dodd, Mead, 1980.

Langston Hughes and Arna Bontemps met in 1924 in New York and established a life-long friendship. They became leading figures in the Harlem Renaissance and, subsequently, two of the most published Black writers in America. Their friendship endured until Hughes' death in 1967. From 1925 to 1967 Bontemps and Hughes exchanged about 2,300 letters. This collection contains about 500 letters. Referring to these letters in a note to his publisher in 1969, Bontemps described them in the following words:

> "All told I am convinced we have the fullest documentation of the Afro-American experience in the new world, artistic, intellectual, covering the mid-20th century, one is likely to find anywhere. The immediate response of two writers to events and conditions that touched their careers."

INSTITUTIONAL HISTORIES

(004L) Moss, Alfred A. Jr. The American Negro Academy: Voice of the "Talented Tenth." Baton Rouge: Louisiana State University Press, 1980.

Founded in 1897, the American Negro Academy was the first national organization established to promote scholarly endeavors among Black Americans. Between 1897 and its demise in 1928, the American Negro Academy published 22 occasional papers and one book. In this well-documented study, Alfred Moss describes the activities of the American Negro Academy.

GENERAL TREATISES, COMMENTARIES, AND ESSAYS

(005L) Bontemps, Arna W. The Harlem Renaissance Remembered. Essays edited with a memoir. New York: Dodd, Mead,

1972.

Bontemps in his nostalgic memoir recreates the milieu and spirit of the Harlem Renaissance through his recollection of personalities and events which shaped the movement. In the subsequent twelve essays, contributors discuss the major writers, dramatists and personalities which gave the Harlem Renaissance its substance.

(006L) Brawley, Benjamin G. The Negro Genius: A New Appraisal of the Achievement of the American Negro in Literature and the Fine Arts. New York: Dodd, Mead, 1937 (Reprinted, New York: Biblio and Tannen, 1966).

In this pioneering work, Brawley documents and discusses the intellectual and artistic achievements of Black Americans from the mid-18th century through the late 1930s in literature, art, music, oratory, drama, and architecture. A bibliography of representative works by Black Americans is included.

(007L) Butcher, Margaret (Just). The Negro in American Culture. Based on materials left by Alain Locke. New York: Knopf, 1966.

Using materials left by Alain L. Locke, Butcher has fashioned this work into a fine comprehensive survey of Afro-American cultural and intellectual history. In historical sequence, it traces the folk and formal contributions of Afro-Americans to American culture from the mid-18th century to the 1950s.

(008L) Cruse, Harold. The Crisis of the Negro Intellectual. New York: Morrow, 1967.

Most observers believe that it is incumbent on the Black American intellectual to develop his or her artistic or professional ability to its highest level as well as to be an effective spokesperson for the masses of Black Americans. In this highly interpretative and analytical study, Harold Cruse discusses the literary, professional, cultural and political activities of leading Black American intellectuals in Harlem from the 1920s through the 1960s in an attempt to illustrate how they used their talents to analyze and articulate the real conditions and aspirations of the Black masses.

(009L) Franklin, Vincent P. Black Self Determination: A Cultural History of Faith of the Fathers. Westport, CT: Lawrence Hill, 1984.

In this unique cultural history, the cultural values which attracted several hundred thousand Afro-Americans to the Garvey Movement of the 1920s are explored. To document Afro-American cultural meanings, Franklin examined contemporary folk narratives, songs, autobiographies, addresses, letters, and essays for statements which illustrated Afro-American cultural values in the early twentieth century and compared them with similar statements found in the narratives of ex-slaves which were collected in the South in the 1930s by the Federal Writers Project. Franklin observes:

> "The objective was not to have the Afro-Americans masses 'speak for themselves,'... But I do believe that these mass voices support an interpretation that better explains mass behavior in the nineteenth and twentieth centuries."

(010L) Gayle, Addison, Jr., ed. The Black Aesthetic. Garden City, New York: Doubleday, 1971.

In this extremely important collection of essays, Black writers and intellectuals consider a major concept in Afro-American intellectual and cultural history; the Black aesthetic. Discussing Black aesthetic theory and its application to music, poetry, drama, and fiction, these essays, published between 1925 and the late 1960s, represent significant contributions to the understanding of Black aesthetics and to Black cultural and intellectual history.

(011L) Gwaltney, John L. Drylongso: A Self-Portrait of Black America. New York: Random House, 1980.

A product of an anthropological field study, this work is a self-portrait of "core Black Culture" in contemporary America. Gwaltney presents the transcripts of interviews which he conducted with over 40 living Black Americans. In these interviews contemporary mass Black culture is explicated as it is perceived by stable working-class Black Americans in pursuit of the same goals which all Americans seek.

(012L) Huggins, Nathan I. Harlem Renaissance. New York: Oxford University Press, 1971.

This study is a highly interpretive analysis of the Harlem Renaissance. It focuses on the years 1920 to 1930. The literature produced in the movement is critically examined by Huggins. He concludes that the Harlem Renaissance was a failure, contending that most of the literature produced during the period is not illustrative of a distinctive Black American voice.

(013L) Lewis, David L. When Harlem Was In Vogue. New York: Knopf, 1981.

Lewis' indepth treatment of the Harlem Renaissance commences in 1905 when white Harlemites began to move to other sections of New York City. Based on original correspondence, numerous interviews, and an examination of a dazzling array of sources, this study gives an insightful and comprehensive interpretation of the Harlem Renaissance. Lewis asserts that the movement, quite contrary to most opinions, was initiated by Black Americans, not white Americans.

(014L) Thorpe, Earl E. The Mind of the Negro: An Intellectual History of Afro-Americans. Baton Rouge, LA: Ortlieb Press, 1961 (Reprinted, Westport, CT: Greenwood Press 1970).

This pioneering study traces the development of Afro-American intellectual thought, as revealed through published works, from the mid-18th century to the late 1950s. Thorpe analyzes the historical progression of expressed ideas and attitudes of Afro-Americans on a variety of subjects such as slavery, religion, democracy, emancipation, plantation life, education, abolition, the presidency, the Washington-DuBois Controversy, Black Nationalism, lynching, the arts and literature, politics, capitalism, socialism, communism, and Black history.

(015L) Van Vechten, Carl. "Keep A-Inchin' Along": Selected Writings of Carl Van Vechten About Black Art and Letters. Edited by Bruce Kellner. Westport, CT: Greenwood Press, 1979.

Photographer, music and dance critic, Carl Van Vechten contributed significantly to the careers of several Harlem Renaissance artists, writers and intellectuals. He established lasting and productive friendships with many of these personalities and other Black creative artists who came to prominence after the Harlem Renaissance. This collection presents Van Vechten's essays and reviews on Black arts; a selection of his correspondence with Black artists writers and personalities between 1924 and 1961; and reproductions of several photographs of Black artists, writers and intellectuals by Van Vechten.

(016L) Voices From the Harlem Renaissance. Edited by Nathan I. Huggins. New York: Oxford University Press, 1976.

This anthology is a collection of writings by Harlem Renaissance personalities who are representative of the "New Negro." Part I presents political writings which reflect "self-conscious social and economic radicalism," Part II contains works by the Harlem Renaissance writers which explore aspects of Afro-American culture. Part III consists of reflections on the Harlem Renaissance by personalities who were active in the movement.

(017L) Waldron, Edward E. Walter White and the Harlem Renaissance. Port Washington, N.Y.: Kennikat Press, 1978.

Walter White was an important Harlem Renaissance personality. Two of White's novels were published during the period: The Fire and the Flint (1924); and Flight (1926). White, a close friend to several Harlem Renaissance writers, was instrumental in arranging publishing contacts for many of these writers. In this absorbing study, Edward E. Waldron focuses on Walter White's role in the Harlem Renaissance.

COLLECTIVE BIOGRAPHY

(018L) Thorpe, Earl E. Black Historians: A Critique. New York: Morrow, 1971.

In the precedent-setting study, the research and scholarship of Afro-American historians are assessed. After discussing the development of Afro-American historiography, Thorpe presents profiles of individual Afro-American historians, documenting their achievement and discussing their philosophies. Historians who were active from the mid-19th century to the 1960s are included.

SELECTED JOURNAL ARTICLES

(019L) Friedman, Murray. "New Black Intellectuals." Commentary 69(June 1980):46-52.

The philosophies on race relations and affirmative action of three controversial Black intellectuals are discussed by Friedman. The Black intellectuals are Thomas Sowell, William Julius Wilson, and Derek A. Bell, Jr.

(020L) Harris, Robert L., Jr. "Coming of Age: The Transformation of Afro-American Histography." Journal of Negro History 67(Summer 1982):107-121.

Prior to the 1960s, Afro-American Historiography lacked a distinctive conceptual framework. Two forces in the 1970s are credited by Harris with propelling a transformation of Afro-American historiography. One was the Black Consciousness Movement. The other was Harold Cruse's Crisis of the Negro Intellectual in which Cruse recognizes:

> "...the centrality of Afro American culture for understanding the contours of Afro-American history."

Harris discusses new developments which have occurred in Afro-American historiography in the last twenty years. He concludes:

> "Afro-American historiography, with its own conceptual and methodological concerns, is now poised to illuminate the Afro-American past in a manner that will broaden and deepen our knowledge of black people in this country."

(021L) Kirby, John B. "Uncertain Context: America and Black Americans in the Twentieth Century." Journal of Southern History 46(November 1980):571-86.

Kirby observes that many recent histories about Black Americans in the 17th, 18th, and 20th centuries are not developed in an integrative framework As examples, he discusses Harlem: The Making of a Ghetto, 1890-1930, by Gilbert Osofsky (1966); and Before the Ghetto: Black Detroit in the Nineteenth Century, by David M. Katzman (1973).

(022L) Meier, August; Rudwick, Wlliott, J. Franklin Jameson, Carter G. Woodson, and the Foundation of Black Historiography. The American Historical Review 89(October 1984):1005-1015.

In the early years of the Association for the Study of Negro Life and History (currently the Association for the Study of Afro-American Life and History), Carter G. Woodson applied to many foundations for funds to put the organization on sound financial footing. J. Franklin Jameson, a leader in the American Historical Association, assisted Woodson in acquiring such funding. Meier and Rudwick detail Jameson's role in enhancing Woodson's efforts to obtain money from the Carnegie Corporation, the Rockefeller philanthropies and other foundations for the research programs of the Association for the Study of Negro Life and History.

SELECTED DISSERTATIONS

(023L) Goggin, Jacqueline A. "Carter G. Woodson and the Movement to Promote Black History." Ph.D. dissertation, University of Rochester, 1984.

With the founding of the Association for the Study of Negro Life and History in 1915 (currently known as the Association for the Study of Afro-American Life and History), Carter G. Woodson laid the foundation for the systematic study and promotion of Black History. Jacqueline Goggin documents Woodson's role and activities on behalf of the promotion of Black History in this study.

(024L) Jubilee, Vincent "Philadelphia's Afro-American Literary Circle and the Harlem Renaissance." Ph.D. dissertation, University of Pennsylvania, 1980.

Although most writers have designated Harlem as the focal point of the New Negro Renaissance of the 1920s, Black communities across the nation were experiencing at the same time an outpouring of Black artistic expression. Jubilee focuses on the literary outpouring of Philadelphia's Black communities during this period.

Subject Index

(Compiled by Rosemary Stevenson, Afro-Americana Bibliographer, University of Illinois, Urbana-Campaign)

Author-Title Index

Compiled by Rosemary Stevenson, Afro-Americana Bibliographer, University of Illinois, Champaign-Urbana)

About the Compiler

DONALD FRANKLIN JOYCE is Coordinator and Associate Professor at the Downtown Campus Library of Tennessee State University. He is the author of *Gatekeepers of Black Culture: Black-Owned Book Publishing in the United States, 1817-1974* (Greenwood Press, 1983) and has contributed articles to *American Libraries* and the *Journal of Library History.*